INTERMEDIATE 2

ENGLISH

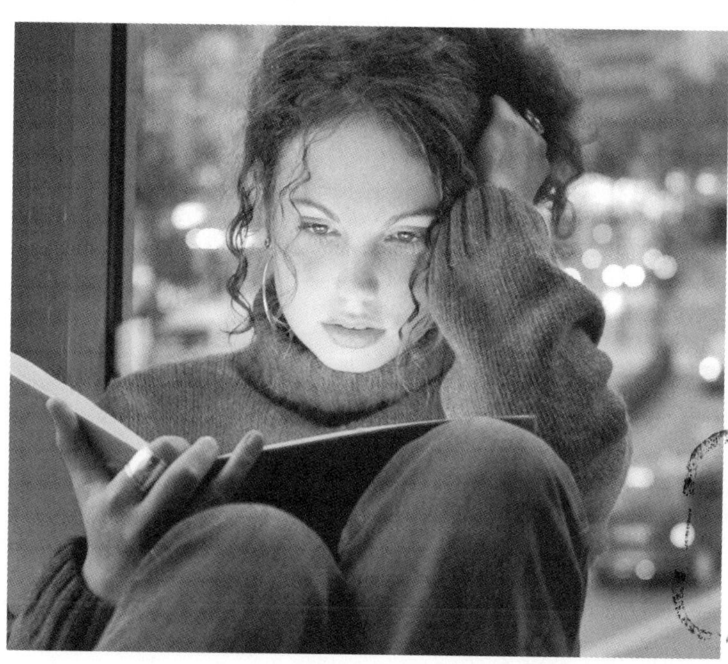

Mary M Firth and
Andrew G Ralston

Hodder Gibson

A MEMBER OF THE HODDER HEADLINE GROUP

The Publishers would like to thank the following for permission to reproduce copyright material:
Photo credits
Sipa Press/Rex Features (page 12); Sipa Press/Rex Features (page 13); Hideo Kurihara/Alamy (page 33); akg-images/Louvre Museum, Paris (page 35); PEANUTS © United Feature Syndicate, Inc. Dist. Knight Features (page 45); Imperial War Museum Q79045 (page 62); donaldcooper@photostage.co.uk (page 93); British Film Institute (page 106); www.bdi-images.com (page 119); 'Breathtaking, whichever way you look at it', Image reproduced with kind permission of Royal Mail, Artwork supplied by Proximity London (page 121).
Acknowledgements
Extracts from question papers are reprinted by permission of the Scottish Qualifications Authority.
A Walk in the Woods © Bill Bryson. Extracted from A WALK IN THE WOODS by Bill Bryson, published by Black Swan, a division of Transworld Publishers. All rights reserved; 'Smile Please', Copyright Guardian Newspapers Limited 2004; 'Rats! We can't be 50', The Herald (Glasgow); "Remote" from *The Great Profundo and Other Stories* by Bernard MacLaverty, published by Jonathan Cape. Reprinted by permission of the Random House Group Ltd.
Illustrations
Linden Artists/Clive Spong (pages 65, 78, 120)
All other illustrations © Moira Munro 2005

Every effort has been made to trace all copyright holders, but if any have been inadvertently overlooked the Publishers will be pleased to make the necessary arrangements at the first opportunity.

The authors would like to thank Mr Simon Easton for his help with the Mass Media section of this book.

Orders: please contact Bookpoint Ltd, 130 Milton Park, Abingdon, Oxon OX14 4SB. Telephone: (44) 01235 827720. Fax: (44) 01235 400454. Lines are open from 9.00 – 5.00, Monday to Saturday, with a 24-hour message answering service. Visit our website at www.hoddereducation.co.uk. Hodder Gibson can be contacted direct on: Tel: 0141 848 1609; Fax: 0141 889 6315; email: hoddergibson@hodder.co.uk

First published in 2005 by
Hodder Gibson, a member of the Hodder Headline Group
2a Christie Street
Paisley PA1 1NB

Impression number 10 9 8 7 6 5 4 3
Year 2010 2009 2008 2007

Cover photo Getty Images/Taxi (Christophe Wilhelm)
Typeset in 9.5/12.5pt Frutiger Light by Phoenix Photosetting, Chatham, Kent
Printed and bound in Great Britain by Martins The Printers, Berwick-upon-Tweed

A catalogue record for this title is available from the British Library

ISBN-13: 978-0-340-90697-2

CONTENTS

AN INTRODUCTION TO INTERMEDIATE 2 ENGLISH

As far as the level of difficulty is concerned, Intermediate 2 English can be regarded as fitting in somewhere between Standard Grade and Higher.

It involves similar types of exercises to those you will have done last year for Standard Grade but the layout follows the pattern of the Higher Paper.

There are various internal assessments – that is, exercises done as part of your school work – which have to be passed before you can proceed to the next stage of the course.

For example, you will be given a textual analysis exercise (usually based on a previously unseen poem) and you will choose a book to read which will form the basis of a personal study.

That part of the course will be covered in school. The purpose of this book is to help you with your preparation for the final exam.

What exactly does the Intermediate 2 exam involve?

There are two papers:

Close Reading, consisting of a passage (usually about two pages in length) with detailed interpretation questions.

You are allowed 1 hour to complete this paper and it is worth 30 marks.

Critical Essay, where you write two essay-type answers from a choice of questions on drama, prose, poetry, film and TV drama, and language. (In practice, most candidates will answer on two texts they have been studying in class.)

You are allowed 1 hour 30 minutes to complete this paper and each question is worth 25 marks.

How do I use this book?

It could be used in the classroom, but you could also use it for individual study. It covers the work that you are doing in class, but presents it in a different way, so that you can read the explanations and work through the practice exercises yourself without the help of a teacher. That's why, in most cases, the exercises are followed by suggested answers.

Of course, you might try and take shortcuts. You might not bother doing the exercises and simply read the answers without attempting your own. Using the book in this way will still be helpful in showing you the types of answers that are required, but it is recommended that you attempt them yourself first so that you can see whether you are understanding the explanations in the text.

This book is divided into two parts, just like the Intermediate 2 exam.

> **Part 1** deals with Close Reading and takes you through the methods required to answer the various types of questions. There are two full-length practice papers, with sample answers.
>
> **Part 2** looks at three typical literature texts and gives an example of a film text and a language topic for the Critical Essay part of the exam. You will be shown how to summarise the main points of the text and how to pick out and discuss technical features. The stages involved in writing a critical essay are explained, from initial planning to final draft. Specimen essays are included to show you examples of pass standard writing.

At the end of the book there is a glossary of language terms that will be useful both for Close Reading answers and for the Critical Essay paper.

PART 1

Paper 1: Close Reading

The first paper in the Intermediate 2 exam is called 'Close Reading'.

You will have *1 hour* in which to complete the paper.

What is Close Reading?

Close Reading is a test of comprehension.

You will be given a piece of **non-fiction** to read. It will be around 1000 words long – that is, roughly two sides of A4 paper. This will be followed by questions testing three things.

Understanding of *what* the writer has said: you must show you have a grasp of the main ideas and important details.

Analysis of *how* the writer has said it: you must be able to identify techniques of style the writer has used to put over the ideas.

Evaluation of *how well the writer has said it*: you must comment on how effective the writer has been, using appropriate evidence in your explanation.

Beating the clock – some advice on timing

In the Intermediate 2 Close Reading paper it is important to watch the clock carefully and to time yourself so that you complete all the questions in the time allowed. Failing to complete the paper is a common reason for failing to pass. Practising past papers using a clock is recommended.

This might be a projected schedule of the exam, if it is from 1–2 p.m.

12.45: Your invigilator will have asked you to be seated in the exam room at least 15 minutes ahead of the official starting time. The test papers will be distributed, and you will be asked to write your name, your date of birth and the name of your school on the front cover of your answer book. You will also be asked to write down the number of the seat you are occupying.

continued ➢

Hints and Tips

Candidates are asked to write down the name of the desk they are occupying so that cases of similarity between candidates' work may be investigated.

NEVER take the risk of glancing at a neighbour's work. If you are suspected of any malpractice of this kind, both parts of your English exam will be declared invalid, and it is possible that *all* your other results will also be declared void.

12.55: In the few minutes while you are waiting for the exam to begin, read the instructions on the cover of the booklet which will remind you of the answer codes: **understanding**, **analysis**, **evaluation**.

1.00: You will be asked to begin precisely at the start of the hour. Try to spend not much more than 5 minutes on your first reading of the text.

1.08: Start reading the questions.

Hints and Tips

In 2004, for example, the questions were numbered 1–13. However, some questions were split into subsections **a** and **b**, requiring 16 separate answers in total. Simple arithmetic will enable you to see that you have only an average of 3 minutes in which to answer each question.

1.20: You should now have completed around a third of the questions (approximately 10 marks' worth).

1.40: You should now have completed around three-quarters of the questions (approximately 22 marks' worth).

1.55: You should now be finishing your last question. Use the last 5 minutes to return to any questions you may have omitted. After writing the other questions you may now have found the answer. If you are still unsure, it is worth making an attempt.

2.00: The invigilator will now call 'time'. You must stop writing at once.

Do	Don't
◆ Make an attempt to answer each question.	◆ Leave blanks or unanswered questions.
◆ Use your own words, even if they seem a bit clumsy.	◆ 'Lift' whole phrases from the text, unless you are asked to 'quote'.
◆ Write a detailed answer if a question is worth several marks.	◆ Spend too long on 1-mark questions.
◆ Quote examples in language questions, especially those on word choice.	◆ Give vague answers in style questions or answer without quoting examples.
◆ Be precise! Deal with each quoted example separately.	◆ Waste time repeating the words of the questions.
◆ Use bullet points to save time.	

READING THE TEXT

Are there any recommended ways of reading the text that will help me pass the exam?

Yes, there are.

- First, read the **introduction**. This will be just a couple of lines at the top, in italics. It is tempting to skip it to save time, and get straight on with reading the text, but the introduction will give you a useful summary of what the passage is about, so it is well worth taking a few seconds to read it carefully.
- Next, read the passage through once, **as quickly as you can**. You may even **skim read** if that is a skill you have practised. This involves reading very quickly, missing out some words or ends of sentences, 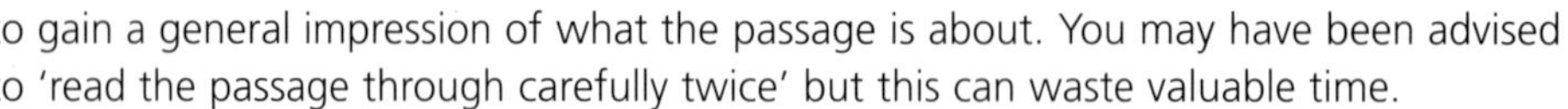 to gain a general impression of what the passage is about. You may have been advised to 'read the passage through carefully twice' but this can waste valuable time.
- 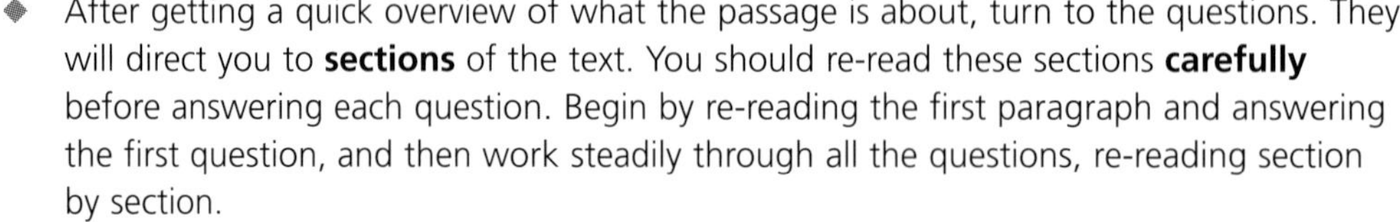 After getting a quick overview of what the passage is about, turn to the questions. They will direct you to **sections** of the text. You should re-read these sections **carefully** before answering each question. Begin by re-reading the first paragraph and answering the first question, and then work steadily through all the questions, re-reading section by section.

ANSWERING THE QUESTIONS

Is there any special way I should answer the questions? I'm not sure if I know all the rules.

It is important that you keep the following four rules in mind.

Rule 1 Use your own words

The very first instruction, which will be written in bold type on the front of your question paper, is to **use your own words as far as possible**. Answering a question by simply 'lifting' a piece of text will get no marks, even if your answer is correct.

Does this mean I can't use *any* of the original words? It's sometimes hard to think of a different one!

No – the rule is not quite as strict as that, you will be glad to know!

Simple, *single* words may be used if there is no obvious alternative, but you must *never* use a complete phrase or group of words exactly as they are used in the original. For example, in the passage 'Smile Please' on pages 33–41, a question asks what made the Eiffel Tower a worthwhile tourist attraction. In the section highlighted for finding the answer, the expression 'an incredible view' is used. In your answer you should not repeat this phrase exactly. Instead, you could say 'a wonderful panorama' or 'you can see a long way from the top'.

Are there any exceptions to the 'use your own words' rule?

Yes. If a question asks you to **quote** or **find an expression in the text** you should copy a word or phrase exactly.

Rule 2 Read the question carefully

Read each question *carefully* to find out what you have to do. Many marks are lost through misreading, or reading just part of the question. Almost every question will **direct** you to a section of text. It is a good idea to highlight the lines or mark them quickly in some way. Your answer *must* be taken from these lines.

Be especially careful with questions that are divided into subsections a, b, c etc. It is very easy to leave one part out by mistake!

Rule 3 Note the number of marks

To the right of the questions in your question paper there are two columns, headed 'Marks' and 'Code'. Always take note of the number of marks in the 'Marks' column. Most questions will be worth only 1 or 2 marks, but some may be worth as many as 4. The length of your answer should be **proportional to the number of marks available**: the higher the number of marks, the longer and more detailed your answer should be. The questions will be set out in the format shown below.

Example

	Marks	*Code*
1 According to the first paragraph (lines 1–7) the two top tourist attractions in Paris are the Eiffel Tower and the Mona Lisa. **In your own words,** explain two reasons why the Eiffel Tower is popular.	2	U

Rule 4 Follow the code

The other column at the right-hand side of the page on your question paper will be headed 'Code'. It will consist of a letter: U, A or E. These letters stand for Understanding, Analysis and Evaluation, and they let you know which of these skills is being tested in the question. Be sure to provide the right sort of answer:

- A U code just asks you to explain the **meaning** of part of the text in your own words.
- In an A answer you must discuss the **style** in which the passage is written.
- For code E, your own **response** to the text is required.

Practising the skills

The following pages will take you step by step through the kinds of questions asked in the Intermediate 2 Close Reading section of the paper. There are also examples for you to try for yourself.

All of the examples are based on past papers. You may find it helpful to use a set of collected past papers alongside this book.

Cracking the codes

Understanding

The main point to remember when answering questions marked U in the Code column is to **use your own words**, even if you feel this seems a bit clumsy. The point is to show that *you* understand what the writer has written.

But will the examiner not take off marks if the expression in my answer is clumsy?

No – your answers are only judged on whether they have actually answered the questions. The quality of your expression is *not* assessed in your answers in the Close Reading paper.

What about my spelling? And punctuation? Won't I lose marks if I make mistakes in those? What about my terrible handwriting? Will they penalise that?

You may be surprised, but again, the answer is 'no' in each case.

Spelling and punctuation are taken into account only in Paper 2: Critical Essay of the Intermediate 2 examination. Errors in spelling and punctuation do *not* affect your marks in Paper 1.

Bad handwriting will not affect your mark *unless* what you write is completely illegible. If your writing falls into this category, it may be possible for you to arrange to use a laptop computer in the exam. You should ask your teacher or tutor about this.

Should I repeat the words of the question in the answer? I was always taught to do that.

No. Repeating the words of the questions wastes time. Answer the question as briefly as you can while still providing the information the question asks for.

Let's now look at a typical 'Understanding' question.

In 2003, the Close Reading passage for Intermediate 2 described a writer's 'fascination with boats' and it began by describing a journey he had made down the Mississippi River.

The first question reads:

	Marks	*Code*
Explain clearly why the writer 'wandered down the Mississippi' in his boat.	2	U

In the text, the answer was contained in this line:

'It was the only possible way of encountering a great river at close quarters.'

Some candidates simply copied out this sentence. They gained no marks.

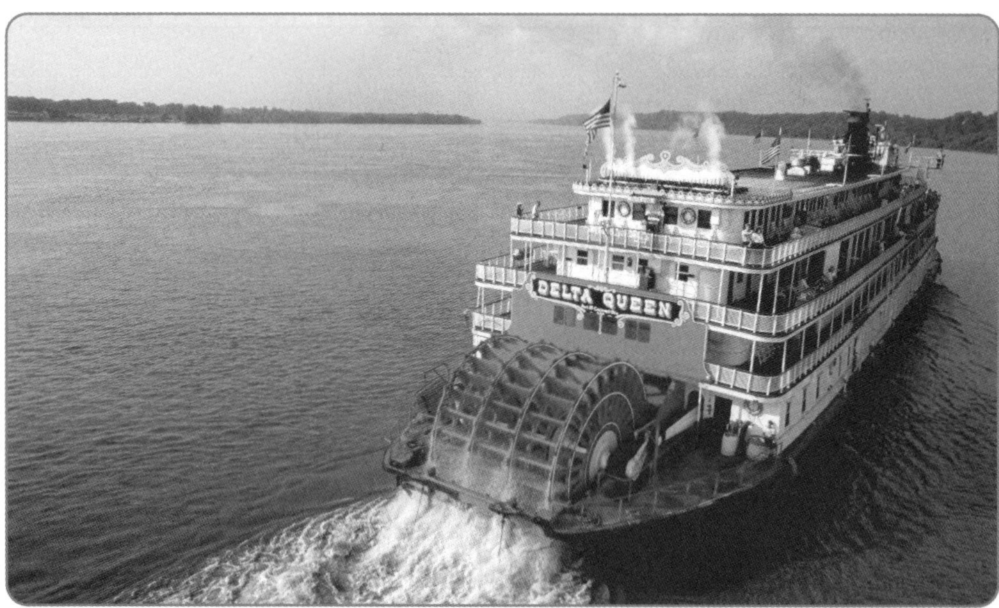

Figure 2.1 A Mississippi paddle steamer

For Practice

The following answers to the question above would gain 2, 1 or 0 marks. Decide what mark you think each would get and why.

a He wanted to see the river at close quarters.

b He could get to know the river well by seeing it from up close.

c The writer wandered down the Mississippi in his boat as it was the only possible way to go.

Turn to page 29 to check your answers.

For Practice

Read the following extract from the 2001 Intermediate 2 Close Reading paper in which the writer described his experiences travelling in a taxi in New York. Then answer the question.

Under other circumstances, I would have taken the subway. Even though everyone knows that the subway will be the first target of terrorists, it's still safer than taking a cab. But I'd been shopping at Balducci's, my favourite New York Deli, and was loath to manoeuvre my bags into the crowded, subterranean world where the sun never shone.

Question

'Under other circumstances I would have taken the subway.'

In your own words, explain the circumstances that prompted the writer to take a cab on this occasion. (2 marks)

Turn to page 29 to check your answers.

Figure 2.2 A New York subway station

Analysis

Questions marked A are likely to seem more difficult. You will be asked to comment on how the writer has expressed an idea but not to explain the idea itself.

Hints and Tips

There are two top tips for answering most Analysis questions successfully:

- **Quote** from the text in your answer.
- **Comment** on your quotation(s).

There are six main areas covered by Analysis questions. In order to explain them it is helpful to divide them into sections, but you will soon see that the sections often overlap. For example, word choice will also be important in discussing 'tone'.

1 Word choice
2 Context questions
3 Figures of speech
4 Sentence structure
5 Linking and general structure
6 Tone

1 Word choice

A word choice question will often ask you to 'quote an expression'. An 'expression' means *either* a single word *or* a phrase (a short group of words). If a **single word only** is required, the question will say so, and you must suggest a **single word**.

Hints and Tips

The golden rule: you should **always use a quotation or quotations** in a word choice answer.

You may be asked for an expression which conveys a particular **shade of meaning**.

For Practice

In the 2003 paper, candidates were asked for a word which meant 'to make a leisurely journey'.

Which of these words do you think was the answer? All are to do with movement. Only one, however, has the right shade of meaning, in containing the idea of 'leisurely'.

a went ☐
b wandered ☐
c travelled ☐

Turn to page 29 to check your answer.

What sort of things are asked about the writer's 'word choice'?

There are a number of frequent topics.

- **Contrast** In the 2004 paper, candidates were asked to show the effect of 'contrasting' word choice. Here it was necessary to select words which were opposites or near opposites. Examples were 'brown' contrasted with 'colourful'.
- **Jargon** This is technical language used by experts in a particular field. Jargon appeared in the text of the 2003 paper about river travel: 'I could gossip comfortably about chutes, sloughs, sawyers, silting-up bends, wingdams and drownings …'.

- **Register** is a term which means a type of language used in a particular setting, or by a particular group of people. In 2001, candidates were asked how the register in one section contrasted with the rest of the passage. In this case the register in the section of the text highlighted was **formal** and it contrasted with the rest of the passage which was in an **informal** register.

Questions frequently test if you can tell the difference between informal and formal language.

The following table will help you to remember the main differences.

Formal	Informal
Complete forms of verbs, e.g. 'I did not'	Abbreviations, e.g. 'I didn't'
Complex, more intellectual words and expressions, e.g. 'inevitable compromise'	Simple, everyday words and expressions, e.g. 'give in'
Longer, more complex sentences; all sentences will be grammatically complete	Short, simple sentences; some sentences may be minor sentences, without verbs, or start with words like 'and' and 'but'
'Literary' punctuation marks, such as semi-colons and colons	Simple punctuation marks such as commas, question marks, full stops and exclamation marks
Standard English, e.g. 'beautiful', 'very important'	Dialect or slang forms, e.g. 'bonnie', 'a big deal'
A distant, impersonal tone	A chatty, friendly tone

Word choice is often important in creating a mood. The use of a large number of positive words will create a cheerful, upbeat impression, while a series of negative words will do the opposite.

Hints and Tips

It is impossible to predict every type of word choice question that might be asked. However, a useful tip is to substitute a simpler, more neutral word for the word or expression the writer has used, and this will often make the special force of the word clearer.

And remember:

- **Quote** examples of words and expressions to illustrate your answer.
- **Comment**, making a separate and precise comment on each example; *do not* just say something vague and general.
- Pick **one example** (quotation + comment) for each available mark.

2 Context questions

'Context' simply means the place where a word or expression is used.

A context question is a special type of word choice question. You must always do two things:

- **Explain the meaning** of the word.
- **Explain the clues** in the text surrounding the word that help you understand the meaning.

For example, the following 'context' question appeared in the 2002 Close Reading paper. The passage was about confronting wild bears in America.

Question

	Marks	Code
Give the meaning of the word 'adroit' and explain how lines 45 and 46 help you to work it out.	2	A

Answer

The sentence that provided the answer was:

'It is foolish to climb a tree because black bears are adroit climbers and you will simply end up fighting the bear in a tree.'

Clearly, the sentence shows that the word 'adroit' means nimble or skilful, since the rest of the sentence reveals that a bear can easily climb a tree in pursuit of someone who tries to escape from it.

For Practice

The following sentence appeared in the same passage.

'Bears are unpredictable, and what works in one circumstance may not work in another.'

Question: **Give the meaning of the word 'unpredictable' and explain how the rest of the sentence helps you to work it out.**

Turn to page 29 to check your answer.

3 Figures of speech

The following four figures of speech appear most frequently in the questions for Intermediate 2:

- **Alliteration** – deliberate repetition of initial consonants in a phrase.
- **Simile** – a comparison of unlike objects using 'like' or 'as'.
- **Metaphor** – a comparison of unlike objects without using 'like' or 'as'.
- **Pun/play on words** – one word having two different meanings creates humour.

Alliteration

Alliteration is a topic of questions in many Close Reading papers.

First, you must be able to recognise an expression such as 'a succession of soft suburban outings' as an example of alliteration. It appeared in the 2003 Close Reading paper which was about sailing.

Question

	Marks	*Code*
What is the effect of the writer's use of alliteration in '... a succession of soft suburban outings'?	1	A

Answer

The answer wanted was that the repetition of the soft 's' sounds had a quiet, soothing effect which conveyed the peacefulness of sailing on the river.

Hints and Tips

Remember: you must always try to explain the *effect* of the sound that is being repeated, not just *identify* it as an example of alliteration.

Help! How can I tell what effect the sounds of the letters have?

Sound is closely related to meaning and tone. Many words, apart from obvious ones like 'buzz', have an element of *onomatopoeia* (where the sound imitates the sense).

- Abrupt, heavy sounds like 'd', 'b' and 'g' are likely to have a punchy, blunt, aggressive tone. 'D' is often the initial letter in words with very negative meanings, such as 'death', 'destruction', 'deadly', 'damned'.
- 'T', 'p' and 'k' are also abrupt, but lighter and sharper sounds. They might indicate neatness or preciseness: 'perfect pike'.
- Words beginning with 'w' seem to have a cold, sad sound, reflecting meanings of words like 'wail', 'wind', 'wet', 'weep'.
- 'F' and 's' are very soft, gentle, whispering sounds which can be pronounced slowly.
- 'l', 'm' and 'n' are smooth, pleasant sounds which can also be prolonged. This group and the previous one often have a positive effect.

Certain combinations of sounds have particular effects, too.

- 'Sl' has a slithery sound and often begins words with unpleasant associations: 'slime'; 'slug', 'slob'.
- 'Cr' has a grating, disturbing note: 'crack', 'crumble'.

When you answer a question on alliteration, try to link the effect of the sound with the meaning. Sometimes, alliteration creates a humorous tone.

For Practice

Pick out an example of alliteration in the following sentence from the passage about bears in America, and comment on its effect.

Nothing unnerved the native Americans more than the grizzly, and not surprisingly since you could riddle a grizzly with arrows – positively porcupine it – and it would still keep coming.

Turn to page 29 to check your answer.

Similes and metaphors

Similes and metaphors both come under the heading of **imagery**. It will always enhance your answer if you identify 'simile' or 'metaphor' correctly using the technical term, spelt correctly. (Simile is the comparison which includes 'like' or 'as'.)

A question on imagery will almost always ask you to do two things:

- Identify the **image**.
- Explain why it is **effective**.

The **image** is whatever thing the comparison is being made to. For example, when a writer describes the experience of camping out at night in 'an inky wilderness', he is comparing his surroundings to ink, which is black and opaque. This is an effective image as it tells us there is no light at all.

Personification is a special type of metaphor, in which an inanimate thing is spoken of as if it were alive.

In the 2003 Close Reading paper on sailing there was a question on imagery.

Question

	Marks	Code
The purpose of lines 41–54 is to illustrate how the wind makes travelling in a small boat an adventure. Giving an example to support your answer, explain how the writer has used *either* sentence structure *or* imagery to do this.	2	A

Answer

The question referred to the following section of the passage:

The wind is a mad travel agent, with a malicious and surrealist turn of wit. You want to go to France – the wind will maroon you for ten days at Dover. You want to go to the Shetland Islands, and the wind will make you spend a week in Bridlington as penance for your vanity. You can't move without the wind's consent, and when you do move, you find yourself suddenly rescheduled, headed for a destination that you hadn't heard of ten minutes ago.

The image used here is an example of personification. The wind is compared to a 'mad travel agent' who sends people to places they don't want to go to and have not heard of. The image of being 'suddenly rescheduled' explains effectively how the changing wind forces the sailor to change his course, just as if a travel agent had sent a holiday-maker tickets to a place he had not chosen to go to.

For Practice

1 The Close Reading paper in 2004 was an account of the experiences of a trainee safari guide in the African bush. He began by describing how everyone feels before a big event:

... as if they had just jumped out of a plane at the start of their first-ever sky dive, and realised they had forgotten their parachute.

Question: Explain how the writer has used imagery to explain how people feel.

Turn to pages 29–30 to check your answer.

2 In the Specimen Close Reading paper (2003) on Science and Scientists, the writer compared people who studied science to:

the rest of us who chose the gentler path of humanities subjects.

Read the following question and then assess the three answers. Only one of the answers is worth 2 marks. Which do you think it is and why?

Question: How does the writer's imagery in this phrase help us understand his attitudes to science and non-science (humanities) subjects?

A **The imagery helps you to understand that the writer thinks humanities subjects are much easier than sciences while sciences are very difficult.**

B **The image of 'the gentle path' helps you understand that humanities are about gentle, kind things, while sciences are about harsher things.**

C **The writer thinks humanities subjects are easier. The image of students of humanities walking up a road which is less steep than the one scientists must walk up makes this clear, as it would require less effort.**

Turn to page 30 to check your answers.

Pun / play on words

A **pun** is a technique in which a word with two different meanings is used to achieve a humorous effect. You may also call a pun a 'play on words', and this is the term to use when an alternative word is used in a well-known phrase to achieve a comic effect.

Such expressions are very popular with writers of newspaper headlines. An article on obesity, for example, was headed:

A FATTY NEW YEAR

Here, a similar sounding word was substituted for the expected word 'happy'.

The title of the 2004 Close Reading passage about a trainee safari guide in Africa was '*Playing at Guide and Seek*'. This was a play on words, substituting 'guide', a word which rhymes with the expected word 'hide', in the common phrase 'hide and seek'.

In addition, the expression 'playing at' was a pun, with the writer using it in the sense of 'pretending or not taking something seriously', rather than the sense of 'playing' like a child.

For Practice

A fashion article in the Glasgow *Evening Times* featured some sixth-year girls from a local secondary school who were photographed looking very glamorous in evening dresses.

The headline attached to the article was:

SCHOOL BELLES

Can you explain how this play on words was appropriate for the article?

Turn to page 30 to check your answer.

4 Sentence structure

The questions that candidates always find hardest are those that ask about sentence structure. However, now is your chance to change this!

What special tips can you give me for answering these questions? Where do candidates go wrong?

Hints and Tips

- Firstly, the most common reason for losing marks is commenting on something that is not sentence structure! Do not discuss ideas, or features such as word choice or alliteration. Even if what you say is true it will get no marks since it will not answer the question being asked.
- Secondly, look at punctuation. Punctuation is a key to sentence structure.
- Thirdly, try to explain the *effect* of the writer's choice of structure; do not simply describe it or identify features such as parenthesis.

The following punctuation marks are likely to be most helpful in answering sentence structure questions.

?	**a question mark** may indicate a simple question or a rhetorical question in which an answer is implied. Questions may affect the tone of the writing, for example by being challenging or emotive (arousing strong feelings in the reader).
;	A **semi-colon** may finish a sentence that is followed by another closely connected or contrasting with it. Semi-colons may also separate items in a list.
,	**Commas** are separating marks. They may separate items in a list, or separate clauses or phrases from the rest of a sentence.
:	A **colon** is an introducing mark. It may introduce a list, an explanation, a quotation, a restatement, an illustration, etc. It always points you *forward* to complete an idea.
...	A group of three dots shows an **ellipsis**. This indicates a tailing off at the end of a sentence, and may imply suspense or an unstated thought.
–	A single **dash** may act like a colon and introduce a list or an additional idea in a sentence. It can also be used at the end of an unfinished sentence, like an ellipsis, but it indicates a more sudden break.
, ... , (...) – ... –	**Pairs** of **commas**, **brackets** or **dashes** around words indicate a parenthesis. This is an addition to the sentence which may give extra information, or make a comment or amendment, or even a joke. The term 'parenthesis' is a useful one to know, as it is extremely common.

In answering a question on sentence structure, consider the following checklist of techniques. The right-hand column shows a typical effect.

A	Long and complex / short simple sentences	Complex sentences may mimic complex ideas; short sentences have impact.
B	Repetition of words or phrases	Repeated ideas will be emphasised or spotlighted.
C	List (may follow a colon or dash)	Provides detail, complexity, etc.
D	Climax / anticlimax following a list	Creates suspense / shows easing of tension.
E	Questions / exclamations / commands	Achieve a particular tone, e.g. emotive (arousing strong feelings).
F	Sentences with no verbs (minor sentences); also called 'note form'	Create a colloquial style or build tension.
G	Unusual word order, e.g. inversion (subject of sentence is delayed)	Alters emphasis; may build tension.
H	Sentences with symmetrical pattern of structure but with contrasting ideas (antithesis)	Provide contrast.
J	Parenthesis	Adds extra information, comment or clarification.

For Practice

Each of the following extracts from former Close Reading passages is an example of one or more of the above techniques. (Some extracts have been adapted slightly.) Can you decide which technique is used each time? In the box write down the letter from the table above which you think is appropriate.

1 *Where do you think you'd get a more satisfactory picture of the safety of Sellafield? The visitors' centre? Or the pub down the road where the boffins knock off for a swifty after work? Exactly.* ☐

2 *When they're tackling questions in the pub, boffins leave the science bit alone because otherwise they see our eyes glaze over. They speak to our concerns as individuals. They generalise. They speculate. They are not rigorous in their explanations. They become unscientific.* ☐

3 *One by one, Dave throws names at me. One by one, I forget them.* ☐

4 *In the case of New York taxis, they have the kind of drivers that are imported for the purpose of scaring you witless. It works.* ☐

5 *Furious, the bear turned and gave chase – despite its lolloping gait, a bear can move at up to 35 m.p.h. – and the two boys scrambled up trees.* ☐

6 *Joe Betts was born in Queens, grew up in Brooklyn and was almost discovered at the 1964 World Fair in New York at which he came second in the Battle of the Bands.* ☐

7 *Dave introduced me to the vast range of skills that a safari guide needs: we've worked on Jeep and boat handling, plant and animal identification, tracking, safety, conservation issues and local politics.* ☐

8 *Only when the taxi was out of sight did I realise he hadn't given me any change.* ☐

Turn to page 30 to check your answers and get an explanation.

5 Linking and general structure

I never seem to get these questions right. How do I answer them?

Learn the right methods!

A very common type of structure question is the so-called 'link' question. It will ask you how one (or occasionally more than one) sentence provides a link between two topics which follow one another.

Why does a writer use linking sentences? What are they for?

A piece of writing would be very disjointed if each new topic followed the previous one without the reader being led into it. The link sentence provides a connection between the topics so that the reader can progress through the whole argument by logical steps.

Example

For example, in the 2002 Close Reading text on the subject of 'Bears', the fifth paragraph began:

So let us imagine that a bear does go for us out in the wilds. What are we to do?

The words 'a bear does go for us' refer back to the previous paragraph in which the author had talked about bears attacking people. The question 'What are we to do?' links forward to the next topic, which is a discussion of the advice given to people who are being attacked.

Hints and Tips

There is a recommended formula to answering a link question, and the above example illustrates it clearly.

Four elements are required:

- **two quotations** from the linking sentence(s), one referring to the previous topic and one to the topic that follows it
- **two very brief summaries** of the topics themselves, in your own words.

For Practice

In the 2004 paper about an amateur African safari guide, the following question was asked:

	Marks	*Code*
Show how the sentence 'That's not what I'm worried about.' is a successful link between paragraphs 3 and 4.	2	A

Paragraph 3 described the danger to the group on safari from armed rebels; paragraph 4 described the narrator's anxiety at having to lead the expedition with his limited knowledge.

Can you select **two** quotations from the designated sentence which could refer to each of these topics?

Turn to page 30 to check your answer.

What other questions might be asked about the structure of a text?

Occasionally, questions will ask you to look at other aspects of structure. Among those that have occurred in previous papers are the following:

- a detailed example
- a short story or anecdote illustrating a point
- conclusion.

Example

The 2003 Specimen paper was about making science more understandable to the general public. It began with a reference to an advertisement for shampoo featuring *Friends* star, Jennifer Anniston, talking about 'science'. This was an 'illustration' of how science is used in everyday life. The term 'illustration' means an example which makes clear some aspect of the text.

6 Tone

What exactly is tone?

Tone is the personal flavour which a writer puts into his writing. Tone will reveal his feelings and his attitude to his topic.

In the Intermediate 2 exam, questions on tone are fairly simple and often involve some form of humour. Of course, it is possible that in future the tone of a passage might be something else, e.g. emotional, depressed, depressing, angry, etc.

However, most of the Close Reading passages have been comic in tone and presented the subject in a humorous way. A common feature of humorous writing is often a chatty, conversational tone.

Example

One of the questions in the 2004 paper was:

	Marks	*Code*
How does the writer establish a conversational tone?	1	A

Another word for 'conversational is 'colloquial'. This means, like the language of everyday speech.

Typical language features which create a conversational tone are:

Feature	Example
Use of abbreviations	I'm
Use of slang and informal expressions	Bit of a surprise, that.
Use of spoken expressions	'Well, thanks'; 'Actually';
Sentence structures such as questions and exclamations which give the impression of chatting with the reader	Don't get me wrong. What are we to do?
Use of exclamation marks	I didn't know this happened!
Use of first person	I think ...
Personal, first person approach	The moment I stepped in the taxi, I knew ...

Additional features of humorous writing include figures of speech, such as:

Irony	Well, thanks.
Hyperbole (exaggeration)	Taxis are airless death-traps.
Alliteration	A moody male.

For Practice

Can you identify the **tone** of the following extracts? Give at least *one* reason for each answer. The tone will be one of the following: informal, chatty, humorous, ironic, tongue-in-cheek.

(In several examples it would be possible to justify more than one of these answers.)

1 *There's so much fascinating stuff to learn about this place, and that's before you've got to the tricky business of remembering what everything is called.*

2 *A revolution is happening in the communications industry: ad copywriters like me are standing back and watching as real people talk to real people. The scandal!*

3 *The moment I stepped into the taxi I knew something was wrong. For a start the driver was called Eddie and taxi drivers in New York shouldn't have names.*

4 *Take it from me, if you are in an open space with no weapons and a grizzly comes for you, run. You may as well.*

5 *'Hey everyone,' I call. I realise that the clients are all looking the other way. It turns out that we are not more than 50 yards from a small herd of giraffe. Actually, it's 100 yards now. Not only was I the last to spot them, my shouting has scared them off.*

Turn to page 31 to check your answers.

Evaluation

Lastly, you must think about questions marked E (for Evaluation) in the Code column. If you look through past papers, you will notice that there are fewer evaluation questions than those marked U or A. However, evaluation questions are worth quite a lot of marks: there is usually one that is worth 4 marks, and another worth 2. Most often, these questions come at the end of the paper. You will find that the understanding and analysis questions will help you in answering the evaluation ones: this is why the evaluation questions are mainly kept until last.

Evaluation basically means deciding how good something is.

Hints and Tips

Rules to follow:

- Always answer **positively**: the pieces of writing will have been chosen for their excellence, and it is up to you to show that you are aware of it.
- Pick out and name **techniques of style**. Useful ones might be hyperbole; imagery; a particular tone, for example a chatty or sarcastic tone; personal reference; colloquial language; contrast; and so on. The pieces chosen for Intermediate 2 are very often light-hearted, and so a reference to humour and how it is achieved will often be relevant.
- Always **quote** to support your answer.
- **Do not be vague**: picking out specific examples will keep you on the right track.

Evaluation questions will ask you to show that a writer has achieved a purpose: the questions will use words like 'entertaining', 'effective', 'enjoyable', 'convincing' and 'appropriate'. In the case of the 4 mark questions, you will be asked to select **two** techniques to explain.

Example

In the 2002 passage by the humorous writer Bill Bryson, the last question read:

	Marks	*Code*
Bill Bryson is a very popular writer of travel books.		
Referring in detail to at least two techniques he uses in this passage, explain why people might find his writing enjoyable.	4	E

For Practice

The following lines comprise the opening paragraph of the Bill Bryson passage.

Through long winter nights in New Hampshire, while snow piled up outdoors and my wife slumbered peacefully beside me, I lay saucer-eyed in bed reading clinically precise accounts of people gnawed pulpy in their sleeping bags, plucked whimpering from trees, even noiselessly stalked (I didn't know this happened!) as they sauntered unawares down leafy paths or cooled their feet in mountain streams. People whose one fatal mistake was to smooth their hair with a dab of aromatic gel, or eat juicy meat, or tuck a chocolate bar in their shirt pocket for later, or in some small, inadvertent way irritate the olfactory properties of the hungry bear. Or, come to that, whose fatal failing was simply to be very, very unfortunate – to round a bend and find a moody male blocking the path, head rocking appraisingly, or wander unwittingly into the territory of a bear too slowed by age or idleness to chase down fleeter prey.

a Find an example of each of the following techniques of style which could be used to answer the question. One example is given to start you off:

Technique	Example
Contrast	Writer's wife 'slumbered peacefully', while he read horrific accounts of bears
Personal reference	
Hyperbole	
A chatty tone	
An ironic tone	
Alliteration	
Word choice	
Listing structure	

Turn to page 31 to check your answers.

b Referring in detail to at least two techniques the author uses in this paragraph, explain why people might find his writing enjoyable.

Turn to page 32 to check your answers.

Answers to Practice Questions on Close Reading

Understanding

Page 12

a This answer gets **1 mark** only. The first part of the answer is correct and put into the candidate's own words and thus gains 1 mark, but the second part of the answer is 'lifted' from the text and is worth 0 marks.

b This answer gains **2 marks**, since both the idea of 'encounter' and 'at close quarters' are put into the candidate's own words.

c This answer gains **0 marks**, as it does not contain either of the ideas of 'encounter' or 'at close quarters'. There is no need to repeat the words of the question.

Page 13

Correct answer for 2 marks: He had been shopping and had bags to carry (1); the subway was always full of people which would have made managing his bags awkward (1).

Answer for 1 out of 2 marks: 'It was an underground, gloomy world without sunlight.' This would gain only 1 mark. Although that might be a reason for a traveller to avoid the subway, the subway is always like that, and therefore it was not the main reason for avoiding it *on this occasion*.

Unacceptable answer: 'The subway is more dangerous than a taxi.' This answer is completely wrong and would gain 0 marks. The writer describes this as a common belief which he knows to be false, as the subway is actually 'safer than taking a cab'. In addition, the prospect of a terrorist attack would be no different on this day.

Analysis

Page 14 (Word choice)

b 'Wandered' suggests going slowly and not always in a direct line.

Page 16 (Context)

'Unpredictable' means 'impossible to tell in advance what they will do'.

This can be worked out, as it says the same tactics do not always succeed with bears on different occasions.

Page 18 (Alliteration)

'positively porcupine it'.

The effect of the short 'p' sounds is to create a sharp, spiky effect which is very humorous in the context, where a bear with arrows sticking in it is compared to a porcupine.

Page 20 (Imagery)

1 Sky-diving is a very daring activity, and doing it for the first time would be nerve-racking. The image suggests, through exaggeration (hyperbole), the nervousness experienced when people undertake a new challenge. Forgetting the parachute would bring the

***Answers** continued* ➢

Answers continued

terror of certain death to the sky-diver. This addition to the image is so extreme that the writer's use of exaggeration becomes humorous. The black humour reinforces the idea of how frightening it feels when you embark on something new, knowing you are not properly prepared, which you expect to end in disaster.

2 Only answer C gains full marks.

- Answer A does not 'identify the image' although it shows understanding of the meaning.
- Answer B misunderstands both the meaning and the image.
- Only answer C identifies the image clearly, which is of climbing paths of varying steepness. This is compared to the difficulty of the subjects.

Page 21 (Pun / play on words)

'Belles' means beautiful girls. The girls in the article are schoolgirls. 'Belles' sounds like 'bells' which are associated with the school day.

Page 23 (Sentence structure)

1 = E, F The questions and minor sentences create a colloquial tone. The last (minor) sentence answers the writer's own question.

2 = B The repetition of 'They' at the beginning of several sentences throws strong emphasis on the scientists and how they respond.

3 = H The two sentences are examples of a balanced contrast (antithesis). Each sentence begins with the same phrase, Dave contrasts with 'I', and the last part of each sentence has the contrasting ideas of giving names and forgetting them.

4 = A The very short sentence contrasts with the one before it to provide impact and humour.

5 = J The parenthesis provides additional information.

6 = D The list ends in an anticlimax by providing a detail which is trivial: 'came second'.

7 = C The list emphasises the large number of things that are being taught.

8 = G This is an example of inversion. We are made to wait for the main piece of information in the sentence, namely that the narrator got no change.

Page 24 (Links)

'That's' refers **back** to the earlier topic of the armed rebels;

'what I'm worried about' links **forward** to the topic of his anxiety over his lack of knowledge.

***Answers** continued* ➢

Answers continued

Page 26 (Tone)

1 = informal Word choice of 'stuff' and 'tricky' is informal; abbreviations 'there's', 'that's' and 'you've' are also informal.

2 = ironic He is being ironic in suggesting it is shocking – 'The scandal!' – that real people should dare to talk to one another, when this is quite normal.

3 = tongue-in-cheek The writer is pretending to be serious but actually is joking when he says that New York taxi drivers 'shouldn't have names'. This is obviously absurd, as is the exaggeration that 'something was wrong' when the driver introduced himself.

4 = chatty The writer is giving the reader orders, such as 'run', and addressing the reader as 'you', as if he is talking.

5 = humorous The idea of the guide being the last to spot the giraffes is funny, as is the fact he has just frightened them off by shouting. His confession of incompetence is humorous.

Evaluation

Page 28

a Possible answers include:

Technique	Example
Contrast	Writer's wife 'slumbered peacefully' while he read horrific accounts of bears; 'noiselessly stalked ... as they sauntered unawares ...'
Personal reference	'I lay ... in bed reading'
Hyperbole	'Saucer-eyed'; 'gnawed pulpy'
A chatty tone	'I didn't know this happened!'
An ironic tone	'fatal mistake ... to smooth their hair with a dab of aromatic gel'; 'to be very, very unfortunate'
Alliteration	'fatal failing'; 'moody male'; 'wander unwittingly'
Word choice	'gnawed pulpy'; 'plucked whimpering from trees'; 'the olfactory properties of the hungry bear'.
Listing structure	'to smooth their hair ..., or eat juicy meat, or tuck a chocolate bar in their shirt pocket ..., or ...'

Answers continued ➢

Answers

b *Specimen answer*

Note: The technical terms used are shown here in **bold type** to draw your attention to them: they should not be underlined or marked in any way when you answer in the exam.

Readers might find Bill Bryson's writing enjoyable as he creates **humour** *in a variety of ways. He uses* **contrast** *to this effect when he describes his wife 'slumbering peacefully' beside him as he reads accounts of bear attacks which make him so scared he is 'saucer-eyed'. This expression, which is an example of* **hyperbole**, *creates a comical picture of Bryson with his eyes widened in terror. The description of the victims who 'sauntered' in idyllic settings like 'leafy paths' and 'mountain streams' contrasts with the horrible fate in store for them: 'gnawed pulpy'. Bryson also uses techniques like* **alliteration** *to produce a* **humorous tone**: *'moody male'. His choice of very* **elaborate words** *to describe something simple also has a comical effect, for example when he says 'olfactory properties' instead of 'sense of smell'.*

Commentary: The above answer refers to more than two techniques, saying just enough about each one, together with an example to ensure gaining a mark for each technique. However, you could discuss fewer techniques in more detail, giving more examples, and this could also gain full marks.

In questions like this, examiners may award marks in various combinations, such as 1 + 1 + 1 + 1, or 2 + 2, or 3 + 1.

Chapter 3

FINDING THE RIGHT ANSWER (I)

The following passage is modelled on the type of Close Reading test which you will have in the Intermediate 2 exam. After each question several possible answers will be given. At least **one** answer will be worth full marks for the question while other answers will be worth less than full marks. Some answers will be examples of bad practice and will be worth no marks. Your task is to decide which of the answers best fits the question. You should award your chosen answer full marks, noting why it gains the marks, and you should then assess the alternative answers.

After you have worked through all the questions and allocated the mark you think each answer deserves, turn to page 42 and compare the comments in the marking commentary with your own assessments.

The passage which follows is adapted from a newspaper article. In it, a journalist tells of spending a day with Leonardo da Vinci's painting, the Mona Lisa.

Figure 3.1 The Louvre Museum

Smile Please

It's the most famous painting in the world and a must-see for anyone visiting Paris. But most people fight through the crowds in the Louvre Museum to spend a mere 15 seconds in front of it – just long enough to grab a snapshot. At least at the Eiffel Tower, the other highlight of travel-brochure Paris, you get the excitement of the lift and an incredible view. Here you get one small, dark picture surrounded by a jostling crowd of hundreds. This year the crowds lining up to see the Mona Lisa have grown thicker than ever. So why do people still come in their thousands to pay homage to the painting?

If you start queuing well before the Louvre's doors open at 9 a.m., and walk briskly through a network of long galleries that stand between the entrance hall and the first-floor room where the painting hangs, you can reach the Mona Lisa at about 9.09, before anyone else. For a short few minutes it is cool and quiet. A guard is rearranging the crowd barriers in the centre of the room with careful precision.

continued ➢

Four Chinese tourists are the first visitors at 9.11. They arrive, visibly delighted, and begin to examine the picture, holding their hands up to shield their eyes against a sun which isn't there. They take a few pictures of the painting and then of each other in front of the painting. Their delight lasts for about 50 seconds, after which they hurry off.

The rumble of approaching feet is already audible by 9.14, as dozens of people make their way rapidly down the grand gallery, rushing past Raphaels and other old masters, including a few other Leonardos, guided by the Mona Lisa sign posts. By 9.20 there is a group of 28 people standing in front of the painting and fathers are already having to hold their children above the crowd so that they can see.

At 9.30 the crowd has grown to about 47. Mobile phones are used to take pictures. Children show their parents how to use the equipment. The noise of the clicking of shutters, the buzzing of zooms whirring in and out, the satisfied pips of the machines, becomes overwhelming. At 10.14 the mass of people is 12 rows deep; 15 minutes later there are so many people elbowing from behind that it becomes uncomfortable to stand at the curved wooden barrier by the front of the picture.

'She must be one of the ugliest women in the world', a teenager mutters.

By midday the room is seething with visitors, the line heaves towards the front, a slow, weary trudge, and around 70 more people file in every minute. Waiting to see the Mona Lisa has all the thrill of standing in an airport check-in queue. Caged in a box of bullet-proof glass, the picture looks unimpressive under the harsh lighting.

Among the thousands who process past throughout the day, there are very few who pause to look hard. Takuya Sejima is an exception, stopping for over 30 minutes. Next to the rushing masses, his behaviour looks eccentric, verging on the insane. An 18-year-old art student from Tokyo, he wants to assess why Leonardo made the left hand so much larger than the right hand, and so out of proportion with the face. 'It's marvellous. It's difficult to express why in words,' he says.

When it was first exhibited in the Louvre in the eighteenth century, it was prized less than many other paintings. But in the nineteenth century the Mona Lisa was seized on by poets as an ideal of womanhood, her smile and eyes venerated. The mystery over who she was increased her allure. Then, just as the painting was gaining mass recognition, it was stolen, in 1911, at a time when popular newspapers were booming. The image was reproduced globally as the search began. Such was the painting's new significance, that people lined up to stare at the empty space where the picture had been hanging. The story of the theft and its rediscovery inspired dozens of books and films.

However, it has been said that the Mona Lisa is the single most disappointing piece of art work in the world. The picture most people have in their minds is much larger and brighter. It is true that the poster reproduction in the museum shop is a much bolder image. With this fresh in your mind, the original looks dour and gloomy. Moonkyou Kim, a tour guide with a group of 16 tourists from Seoul says, 'People aren't very happy

continued ➢

when they see it. It's too small. They don't believe it's the original.' But of all the people I approach over the day, the majority still say the picture is wonderful and they are thrilled to have seen it.

Later the tourists become wearier, their legs heavier, more prone to squabbling with their partners. The number of tour groups dwindles. The number of French visitors increases.

By 9.30 p.m. there are only about 10 people left in the room, and for the first time all day there's time to really examine the painting. But as closing time approaches, guards shoo the remaining visitors away so that only Mohamed Elabdi, the night cleaner, remains sweeping away the mound of rubbish discarded over the day at the foot of the painting. After 30 years in France, he saw the painting for the first time three days ago when he started this new job with the Louvre. 'It's hard to understand what the fuss is about,' he says. 'But the way that the eyes follow you around the room as you work is disconcerting.'

Questions and Answers

	Marks	Code
1 According to the first paragraph (lines 1–7) the two top tourist attractions in Paris are the Eiffel Tower and the Mona Lisa. **In your own words**, give two reasons why the Eiffel Tower is popular.	2	U

Answers

- *A The Eiffel Tower has the excitement of the lift and an incredible view.* ☐
- *B The Eiffel Tower has a lift which is exciting and you get an excellent view from it.* ☐
- *C The Eiffel Tower is popular as it is thrilling to go up it in the lift and from the top you can enjoy looking down at the beautiful city beneath.* ☐

	Marks	Code
2 Which expression in the first paragraph suggests that visitors have unusual respect for the Mona Lisa?	1	A

Answers

- *A pay homage* ☐
- *B fight through the crowds* ☐
- *C come in their thousands* ☐

	Marks	Code
3 In paragraphs 2, 3 and 4 (lines 8–22), the writer gives many precise times: '9 a.m. 9.09, 9.11, 9.14 …'. Explain how this helps the reader imagine the way the visitors come into the gallery in the morning.	2	A

Answers

- *A It gives the impression that they try to be very quick to get a good view since there are not many minutes between each time.* ☐
- *B Such precise times suggest that the visitors plan their visit carefully like a military campaign in order not to miss a second and to beat the other tourists.* ☐

Questions and Answers

	Marks	Code
4 Look again at lines 13–17.		
Explain, with close reference to the text, how the writer achieves a mocking tone in his description of the Chinese tourists.	2	A

Answers

A *The writer mocks the Chinese tourists as they hold up their hands in front of the painting as if before an invisible sun. This suggests the painting is of dazzling beauty but we are told the picture is actually rather dark. The detail of them taking 'a few pictures of the painting and then of each other in front of it' is mocking as it suggests they don't really care about it as they stand with their backs to it and stand in front of it in the photos. The short time they spend, 'about 50 seconds', probably exaggerates how quickly they lose interest and leave.* ☐

B *The writer says the Chinese visitors are 'the first tourists', showing they are too keen which mocks them. 'Holding their hands up to shield their eyes' is mocking as they could not see the picture if they did that.* ☐

	Marks	Code
5 'rushing past Raphaels and other old masters, including a few other Leonardos' (lines 19–20)	2	U
Explain what the writer suggests here about the visitors' appreciation of art.		

Answers

A *The alliteration 'rushing past Raphaels' emphasises the speed and shows the visitors really appreciate art as they want to reach the Mona Lisa so quickly.* ☐

B *The other paintings were mostly old and so the visitors did not appreciate them very much.* ☐

C *The visitors did not genuinely appreciate art since they ignored many other wonderful paintings to rush to the Mona Lisa just because it was famous.* ☐

	Marks	Code
6 Look at lines 24–28.		
Explain, with close reference to the text, how the writer's word choice uses sound effectively to convey the scene in front of the painting.	2	A

Questions and Answers

Answers

A *People were making a lot of noise as their cameras were 'clicking', 'buzzing' and 'whirring'. This noise got on people's nerves: he says it was 'overwhelming'.* ☐

B *The writer uses words which sound like their meaning (a technique called onomatopoeia). Examples are 'clicking', 'buzzing', 'whirring' and 'pips'. The large number of these words with many different sounds helps give the impression of a loud, irritating mixture of mechanical noises from the cameras.* ☐

	Marks	*Code*
7a Pick **two** single words from the first sentence of paragraph 7 (lines 30–31) which best convey the unpleasantly crowded conditions in the gallery at midday.	2	A

Answers

A *seething; heaves* ☐

B *slow; weary* ☐

C *seething; seventy* ☐

	Marks	*Code*
7b Identify the **tone** the writer uses in his comment 'Waiting to see the Mona Lisa has all the thrill of standing in an airport check-in queue' (lines 31–32).	1	A

Answers

A *sarcastic* ☐

B *bored* ☐

	Marks	*Code*
8 Show how the sentence 'Among the thousands who process past throughout the day, there are very few who pause to look hard' (lines 34–35) is a successful link between paragraphs 7 and 8.	2	A

Answers

A *The reference to the 'thousands' of visitors links back to the description of the seething crowds in the previous paragraph. The reference to the 'few who pause to look hard' links ahead to the example which follows of the Japanese art student who is one of the 'few'.* ☐

B *The writer has said that there are large crowds of visitors but most of them rush past and don't appreciate the painting.* ☐

Questions and Answers

	Marks	Code
9 Look again at the account of the Japanese art student, Takuya Sejima (lines 35–39). Explain **two** ways in which he appears different from most other tourists.	2	U

Answers

A *Takuya Sejima stops for over 30 minutes. He looks eccentric, verging on the insane.* ☐

B *Takuya Sejima spends half an hour studying the painting instead of rushing away in a few minutes. He shows genuine interest and knowledge of the composition of the painting, whereas most tourists just take a photograph and leave.* ☐

	Marks	Code
10 Look at lines 40–48.		
In your own words, explain four stages by which the Mona Lisa became world-famous.	4	U

Answers (choose 4)

a *Before the nineteenth century the Mona Lisa was not especially well thought of among the gallery's many other great paintings.* ☐

b *Particular interest began in the nineteenth century when poets started regarding it as a standard of female beauty.* ☐

c *These poets focused attention on the special charm of her smile and her eyes which began to be almost worshipped.* ☐

d *The fact that the identity of the woman in the painting was unknown made it even more intriguing.* ☐

e *The theft of the painting in 1911 was given worldwide press coverage.* ☐

f *Tabloid newspapers had just started and gave huge publicity to the theft.* ☐

g *The bizarre behaviour of the public in coming to stare at the 'empty space' continued to build up the hype around the painting.* ☐

h *The publicity from the theft and the later recovery of the picture sparked off books and films featuring it, which made it a phenomenon.* ☐

	Marks	Code
11 Look at lines 49–55.		
Give **one** reason for visitors finding the painting of the Mona Lisa disappointing.	2	U

Questions and Answers

Answers

A *The actual painting is smaller and dimmer than poster reproductions of it.* ☐

B *People are disappointed because they think it is a fake.* ☐

	Marks	Code
12 In lines 58–60, the writer describes how the tourists become weary and begin to thin out later in the day. Comment on any **one** feature of the sentence structure in these lines which reinforces the ideas in the paragraph.	2	A

Answers

A *The use of the list of comparatives in the first sentence – 'wearier … heavier … more prone …' – mimics the effort needed as the tourists drag themselves through the gallery. The second and third sentences are very short and simple, suggesting the reduction in numbers. They are parallel in structure, with the same opening phrase, creating a monotonous effect, suggesting that interest is fading.* ☐

B *The tourists are now very tired – 'wearier' – and their legs are sore and feel heavy. Because they are tired they become irritable. The writer says the number of tourists 'dwindles' which means gets less.* ☐

	Marks	Code
13 The article ends with an account of the guards ushering the last visitors out and the night cleaner sweeping up rubbish that has been discarded.	2	E

How effective do you find this as a conclusion to the passage?

In your answer you may wish to consider **one** feature such as word choice, contrast, or direct speech.

Answers

A *It is an effective conclusion. The word choice of 'shoo' is effective as it suggests the guards have little respect for the tourists as they treat them like chickens or stray animals. This is comical and quite appropriate as most of the tourists have seemed rather silly and thoughtless and showed no real interest in the art apart from the Mona Lisa.* ☐

B *It is an effective conclusion. The image of the cleaner having to sweep up a large amount of rubbish contrasts with the idea of a beautiful painting in a famous art gallery. It reinforces the idea of the crowds of stupid tourists who treat it as a day out and don't really appreciate the painting.* ☐

Questions and Answers ?

C *It is an effective conclusion. The words of the cleaner act as a summing up of two main attitudes to the Mona Lisa. One attitude is that it doesn't deserve all the attention, while the other is that there is something mesmerising about it. The words thus neatly give both views when he says he doesn't understand the 'fuss' but that he also feels uneasy as he senses her watching him.* ☐

	Marks	Code
14 In what ways might 'Smile Please' be considered a particularly appropriate title for this article?	2	E

Answers

A *It is appropriate because the Mona Lisa is a picture of a woman smiling.* ☐

B *It is appropriate as it has two meanings which are both contained in the passage. 'Smile Please' is traditionally said when you take someone's photograph, and the tourists are described as constantly taking photos both of themselves and of the painting. The lady in the portrait is also most famous for her smile, and so it refers to her almost jokingly, as if she is smiling for the cameras.* ☐

Total marks: 30

Commentary on answers to 'Smile Please'

Question 1

Did you identify the 2 mark answer here? It was answer C. All of the answers showed that the candidate had understood the question and the text. However, answer A would gain no marks, because it has ignored the instruction to 'use your own words'. Almost the whole answer has been 'lifted' unchanged from the text. Answer B is better, as the candidate has tried to use his own words, but it still uses too many of the original words, such as 'view' and 'exciting' which is too close to 'excitement'. Only answer C definitely deserves 2 marks. The candidate has explained the two reasons clearly using different words from those in the original text. It is acceptable to use the word 'lift' in the answer as there is no obvious alternative.

Question 2

The correct answer for 1 mark is A: 'pay homage'. To 'pay homage' means to give a public show of respect or honour and is an example of personification. The other answers reflect the keenness of the visitors, but they do not include the idea of 'respect'. They would each score 0.

Question 3

Answer B is a very perceptive answer which also picks up the slightly mocking tone of such precise times by comparing them to a military campaign. It deserves 2 marks. Answer A deserves 1 mark. It gets across the general idea of having to rush into the gallery, but it doesn't fully appreciate the ridiculously precise timings.

Question 4

I hope you chose answer A here! It makes three good points: firstly noting the irony of shading their eyes although the painting is not at all bright; secondly, the foolish way they stand in front of the painting in the photos, so they are not looking at it, and covering it up; and thirdly, that they rush off in less than a minute. This answer is clearly worth full marks (2). Did you think that answer B deserved any marks? Neither of the reasons given in B was valid. The fact that these tourists were in first was simply stated as a fact by the author. The second point shows the candidate has misunderstood 'shield your eyes', which means to shade your eyes as if from a bright light, not cover them up. So answer B is worth 0.

Question 5

Answers A and B are worth 0. Answer B misunderstands 'old masters', which means great paintings of the past. Neither appreciates the writer's irony in observing that the visitors ignore the other great works of art in the gallery as they rush to see the Mona Lisa. Alliteration is used, but it has a rather mocking tone. Answer C is correct, for 1 mark.

Question 6

Did you pick answer B here? Although answer A quotes words which are examples of onomatopoeia, it does not show awareness of it as a technique. The answer talks about sounds in the gallery, but not the writer's *use of sound* in the word choice. Answer B clearly shows understanding of the technique and it would still have gained 2 marks, even if the name of the technique had not been given in brackets.

Question 7a

The correct choices are 'seething' and 'heaves'. Both imply huge, jostling crowds. 'Weary' and 'slow' describe the effect of the crowded conditions, which is not what is asked. Only answer A gains 2 marks; B gains 0 marks and C, 1 mark.

Question 7b

A – 'sarcastic' gains 1 mark. The writer is writing tongue-in-cheek, as we all know that standing in check-in queues in the airport is far from exciting. 'Boring' describes the waiting, not the tone of the writer, and so gains 0 marks.

Question 8

Answer A is a model answer to a link question. It selects a quotation from the designated sentence, 'thousands', and explains how it links back to a topic in the previous paragraph, namely the huge crowds. It then identifies another quotation, the 'few who pause to look hard', which sums up the topic to follow, and explains what this topic is, namely the keen art student who is an example of 'the few'. Answer B would gain 0 marks since it does not quote from the designated sentence and it does not identify the two linked topics.

Question 9

I think you would have no difficulty in selecting the right answer here! Answer B gives two clear, valid points, using the candidate's own words, and is worth 2 marks. However, in the case of answer A, although the first point is valid, it is 'lifted' directly from the passage. The second point shows he has misunderstood the ironic tone of the writer who does not really think the art student is 'insane'. It is also a direct quotation. This answer is worth 0 marks.

Question 10

This was a trick example! All eight of these points are valid, and all are in the candidate's own words. Therefore, any four, in the right order, with a spread from early to modern times, would gain 4 out of 4 marks.

Question 11

Answer A is the correct one for 1 mark. B is the mistaken belief of some tourists, but it is not a real reason for feeling let down. It would score 0 marks.

Question 12

Answer A is an excellent answer which makes three good points, and therefore has more than enough for the full 2 marks. It addresses the idea of structure and uses grammatical terms like 'listing', 'repetition' and 'use of comparatives'. It looks at sentence length and how the sentences are put together and links this to the ideas. Answer B may appear to be correct, but would get 0 marks. It does not say anything about sentence structure, but merely explains the ideas of the paragraph. It has treated the question as if its code were U (Understanding) and not A (Analysis).

Question 13

Any of these answers would gain full marks. Each is a good example of the amount of detail and explanation required for 2 marks. Each focuses on one of the areas suggested by the question.

Question 14

Answer A is too thin to gain full marks, as it hardly attempts any discussion. It would be likely to gain no more than 1 mark. B is a perceptive answer with enough detail for 2 marks. However, since it is the last question, many candidates may not leave enough time to write as much as this.

Chapter 4

FINDING THE RIGHT ANSWER (II)

In this passage, journalist Miles Fielder discusses why the famous Peanuts comic strip by Charles M. Schulz is so popular.

As with the Mona Lisa passage, sample answers to the Peanuts Close Reading paper are provided. This time, though, you will also find advice on how these answers were worked out.

To make the best use of this material, you should first attempt all the questions on your own.

In the Intermediate 2 exam, you are allowed 1 hour to complete this paper. Practise doing it in that time.

Rats! We can't be 50

When it debuted in an American newspaper in October 1950, the four-frame strip Peanuts introduced a cast of unusually mature kids – Charlie Brown, Lucy, Linus, Peppermint Patty, Schroeder and an extraordinarily smart dog named Snoopy – who have since become cultural icons the world over.

For more than fifty years Charles M. Schulz wrote and drew this funny, poignant, deceptively simple strip, one for each day of the week plus a Sunday edition – more than 18,000 in all.

Beginning in April the entire strip collection will be republished in 'The Complete Peanuts' – 25 books appearing at the rate of two each year over the next 12½ years. It's a mammoth task, the biggest ever undertaken by the Seattle, Washington-based comic book publishing house Fantagraphics.

When Schulz died in February 2000, on the night before the publication of his final strip, newspaper editors made the decision to put Peanuts into syndication, indefinitely.

The most popular comic strip in the world – it's a grand claim, but one the statistics bear out. Peanuts has been published in 21 languages in 2600 newspapers around the globe (some of which have run the strips for 36 consecutive years), garnering a towering readership of 355 million. Schulz's annual earnings rocketed to $50m (£26m).

continued ➢

Some years back *Forbes* magazine put Schulz in its top-10 highest-paid entertainers, along with Bill Cosby, Michael Jordan and Michael Jackson.

A poll run in America in 2002 found Peanuts to be one of the nation's most recognisable cartoon properties, identifiable by 94% of the US public, just two percentiles behind Mickey Mouse. To give this a more modern perspective, The Simpsons polled at 87% and Spiderman at 75%.

So why is Peanuts so popular? Although Schulz recognised the strip's success – he once quipped: 'I did expect it, because it was something I had planned for since I was six years old' – he steadfastly refused to analyse the reasons behind it. His widow, Jean, does, however, offer an explanation for Peanuts' popularity. 'His characters speak of a universal desire to be loved.'

The universal nature of that theme, combined with the deceptive simplicity of the dialogue and drawing, accounts for Peanuts' appeal. Add to that dashes of smarting humour and Schulz's masterstroke of peopling the strip with 'grown-up kids' and you can see why Peanuts has travelled (and aged) so well.

Jean Schulz also attributes Peanuts' popularity to how much of himself Schulz put into it. Charlie Brown is supposed to be an Everyman, but Charlie Brown is also Charles Schulz. The famous gag in which Lucy pulls the football away just as Charlie is about to kick it was inspired by a sporting failure Schulz experienced as a kid (pitching a no hit, no run game of baseball). Charlie Brown's famous melancholic outlook on life, offset with a resolve to get on with it, regardless of how many footballs he fails to kick, is also a reflection of his creator.

In many ways Schulz had a good, solid, comfortable life: the only child of devoted parents, he worked his way through art school, joined the army to fight in the Second World War, had two marriages and five kids. But although Schulz had devoted parents, as a kid he said he felt unloved by everyone other than them. And there was tragedy in Schulz's life – his mother died young of the same cancer that would eventually take her son.

Schulz once said: 'If you want to know who I am, read the strips.'

All the more reason, then, to celebrate the work of a man who gave so much pleasure to so many people for so many years. Schulz refined the art of cartooning, honing the simple lines and slight incident storytelling to nothing less than perfection. And Schulz achieved all this with no great ostentation. He once said: 'A cartoonist is someone who has to draw something different every day and yet draw the same thing over and over.'

Questions

?

1 In your own words, give two facts about the Peanuts cartoons which the author includes in lines 1–10. (2 marks) U

2 The author uses a mix of very informal and very formal styles in the passage. From the first paragraph, pick out one word or one expression which is an example of each. (2 marks) A

3 Explain what the writer means when he says that Charles M. Schulz's comic strips were 'deceptively simple' (lines 13–14). (2 marks) U

4 In paragraph 2 (lines 11–15) the writer emphasises the large number of cartoons Schulz produced. Explain how his use of the dash in line 14 contributes to this. (2 marks) A

5a In line 22 Peanuts is described as 'the most popular comic strip in the world'. How is this claim backed up in the rest of the paragraph (lines 22–27)? (2 marks) A

b 'Schulz's annual earnings rocketed to $50m (£26m).' (line 25)

'Rocketed' means 'increased greatly'. Explain why 'rocketed' is a more effective expression. (2 marks) A

6a Identify Schulz's tone in 'I did expect it, because it was something I had planned for since I was six years old.' (lines 33–34). (1 mark) A

b Select a word from the same paragraph which also relates to this tone. (1 mark) U

7 'So why is Peanuts so popular?' (line 32)

a Show how this sentence is a successful link between paragraphs 6 and 7. (2 marks) A

b From the rest of this paragraph (lines 32–36), explain in your own words why Jean Schulz believed the Peanuts cartoon was so popular. (2 marks) U

8 Explain the image involved in 'Add to that dashes of smarting humour' (lines 38–39) and show how it helps to make the author's point clear. (2 marks) A

9 'Charlie Brown is also Charles Schulz' (lines 42–43). Explain in your own words one example of Schulz's own experience which found its way into the cartoon strip. (2 marks) U

10 Read lines 48–53. By referring to word choice, show how the author builds up both admiration and sympathy for Charles Schulz in these lines. (4 marks) A

Questions *continued* ➢

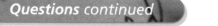

Questions continued

11 In this passage the writer's main purpose is to explain why the Peanuts cartoon strip has been so successful.

By referring closely to the text, clearly explain which of his reasons you find the most convincing. (4 marks) E

Total marks: 30

What to do next

Now check your own answers against the sample answers which follow.

Working through the questions

Question

1 In your own words, give two facts about the Peanuts cartoons which the author includes in lines 1–10. (2 marks) U

Often the first question in a paper is a straightforward, factual one to get you off to a good start! Possible answers here, for 1 mark each, would be:

- The cartoon involves four children who behave in a very grown-up way.
- There is an extremely clever dog called Snoopy.
- Each cartoon contains four pictures.
- Peanuts first appeared in America.
- Peanuts first appeared in 1950.
- The characters are famous throughout the world.

Note that the question asks you to answer *in your own words*. As the question is relatively easy, answers 'lifted' straight from the passage would gain 0 marks.

Question

2 The author uses a mix of very informal and very formal styles in the passage. From the first paragraph, pick out one word or one expression which is an example of each. (2 marks) A

Because Close Reading passages are 'unseen', people generally think that there isn't much revision that can be done to prepare for them. There is some truth in that as far as the Understanding questions are concerned, but you *can* prepare for the Analysis questions by learning such things as figures of speech, language terms and the functions of various punctuation marks.

Question 2 is a case in point. This question is really testing that you know the difference between informal and formal language (explained on page 15). Thus 'kids' would be an example of informal language whereas 'cultural icons' is formal.

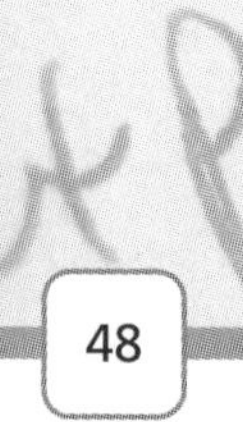

Question

3 Explain what the writer means when he says that Charles M. Schulz's comic strips were 'deceptively simple' (lines 13–14). (2 marks) U

This question is designed to find out whether you know the meaning of the word 'deceptively'. But don't forget to explain 'simple' in your own words as well.

Occasionally there are questions like this which depend on your knowledge of a certain word. If you don't know what it means, look at the **context** (i.e. the words in the rest of the sentence or paragraph) to see if there are any clues. It must be admitted, though, that this doesn't always help. In such cases there isn't much you can do other than guess!

The dictionary gives a definition of 'deceptive' as 'liable to deceive; easily mistaken for something else.'

In the light of this, how would you rate each of these attempts at an answer?

Answers

(i) 'Deceptively simple' means that the comic strips weren't really simple.

(ii) 'Deceptively simple' means that although the comic strips appeared to be straightforward and undemanding, in reality they were more complicated than they looked.

(iii) 'Deceptively simple' means that although the comic strips looked simple the reader could be deceived by this.

(i)	This candidate has not used his own words. He probably does understand what 'deceptively simple' means, but has not given enough explanation.	0 marks
(ii)	'Straightforward and undemanding' is a good explanation of 'simple'. The use of the words 'appeared to be' and 'than they looked' shows that the writer knows what 'deceptively' means. A good answer!	2 marks
(iii)	This candidate certainly understands what the expression means but the explanation relies too much on the words 'simple' and 'deceive'.	1 mark

Question

4 In paragraph 2 (lines 11–15) the writer emphasises the large number of cartoons Schulz produced. Explain how his use of the dash in line 14 contributes to this. (2 marks) A

Again, it is worth revising the functions of punctuation marks such as dashes, colons and semi-colons in order to answer questions like this (see page 22).

An answer like:

Answer

The single dash is used to introduce the total number of cartoons Schulz produced.

describes *what* the dash does but it doesn't really explain its effect. A fuller 2 mark answer might read:

Answer

The dash introduces a pause before giving the total number, making the reader realise just how huge Schulz's output of cartoons was.

Question

5a In line 22 Peanuts is described as 'the most popular comic strip in the world'. How is this claim backed up in the rest of the paragraph (lines 22–27)? (2 marks) A

Your answer should refer to the writer's use of statistics. At least two examples should be quoted or referred to.

Answer

- more than 18,000 in all
- Peanuts has been published in 21 languages in 2600 newspapers
- a towering readership of 355 million
- identifiable by 94% of the US public
- Schulz's position as one of the ten highest-earning entertainers is also evidence of how popular his cartoons were

Question

5b 'Schulz's annual earnings rocketed to $50m (£26m).' (line 25)

'Rocketed' means 'increased greatly'. Explain why 'rocketed' is a more effective expression. (2 marks) A

There is usually at least one question of this type, asking you to think about the associations or connotations of a word rather than its meaning alone.

Recognition that the word 'rocketed' is metaphorical would be a useful starting point. Think about what you associate with a rocket. The main things will probably be speed and travelling upwards. An acceptable answer might be along the lines of this one:

Answer

A rocket travels in an upward direction very quickly. The choice of the word 'rocketed' is therefore effective because it suggests that Schulz's earnings increased extremely quickly. (2 marks)

Questions

6a Identify Schulz's tone in 'I did expect it, because it was something I had planned for since I was six years old.' (lines 33–34). (1 mark) A

b Select a word from the same paragraph which also relates to this tone. (1 mark) U

The concept of tone was explained on pages 25–26. Remember that tone refers less to the meaning of the words than to the way in which they are said.

In this example, the tone could be described as joking, tongue-in-cheek or humorous. The answer to question 6b would therefore be 'quipped', which means to make a witty or amusing remark.

Question

7 'So why is Peanuts so popular?' (line 32)

a Show how this sentence is a successful link between paragraphs 6 and 7. (2 marks) A

Hints and *Tips*

In answering a question on a linking phrase or sentence, always show how it links back to the previous paragraph and forwards to the next one.

Always *quote* from the linking section.

Here are two possible answers to **7a**. How good are they?

Answers

(i) The sentence looks backwards to the points explained in the previous paragraph and the second part looks ahead to the points explained in the next paragraph.

(ii) The words 'so popular' refer back to the previous paragraph which had provided statistics to show that the comic strip was very well-liked. The question 'why' points forward to the rest of the paragraph and to subsequent paragraphs which offer reasons for this popularity.

(i)	This sounds quite good, but in fact it merely repeats the question and gives no detail at all.	0 marks
(ii)	This explains the linking function of both parts of the sentence and also makes clear exactly which previous and following ideas are referred to. The answer quotes the expressions which point to these ideas.	2 marks

Question

7b From the rest of this paragraph (lines 32–36), explain in your own words why Jean Schulz believed the Peanuts cartoon was so popular. (2 marks) U

The line references give away the answer: 'His characters speak of a universal desire to be loved.' Any answer which simply quotes these words will obviously score no marks. This one has to be in your own words!

First, identify the key words: 'universal', 'desire', 'loved'.

Then try to think of close equivalents of these (**synonyms**).

- *Universal*: widespread, common, entire, general
- *Desire*: wish, longing, need, yearning
- *Loved*: cared for, prized, respected, treasured

Hints and Tips

A thesaurus, either in book form or in a computer, is a useful tool when practising answers to this kind of question (although you won't have access to one during the exam).

Possible answer:

Answer

She believed the cartoon was so popular because its characters expressed the longing to be cared for that is common to everyone. (2 marks)

Less successful candidates might only put part of the sentence into their own words:

Answer

She believed the cartoon was so popular because its characters shared the universal longing to be loved. (1 mark)

Question

8 Explain the image involved in 'Add to that dashes of smarting humour' (lines 38–39) and show how it helps to make the author's point clear. (2 marks) A

Imagery is a term that refers to figures of speech involving comparisons, such as simile, personification and metaphor (see pages 18–20).

In a question of this type, you should first work out what is being compared to what. The expression 'Add … dashes of …' refers to a recipe in which an extra ingredient like sauce or spice is added to improve the flavour. Here, the 'smarting [i.e. sharp] humour' adds 'flavour' to the cartoon.

A 2 mark answer might read as follows:

Answer

The author compares the cartoon to a recipe. An ingredient like a few drops of sauce might be added to improve the flavour of the dish; in the same way, the sharp humour adds to the reader's enjoyment of the cartoon.

Question

9 'Charlie Brown is also Charles Schulz' (lines 42–43). Explain in your own words one example of Schulz's own experience which found its way into the cartoon strip. (2 marks) U

This is fairly straightforward. Refer to lines 43 to 45 and remember to use your own words.

Possible answer:

Answer

A disastrous game of baseball played by Schulz as a boy was the inspiration behind the story of Lucy moving the ball and preventing Charlie Brown kicking it. (2 marks)

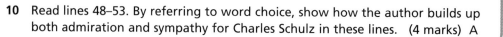

Question

10 Read lines 48–53. By referring to word choice, show how the author builds up both admiration and sympathy for Charles Schulz in these lines. (4 marks) A

As there are four relevant points here, it is best to assume that this answer will be marked on a 'one point – 1 mark' basis.

Quote four examples of word choice and comment on how each one arouses admiration or sympathy in the reader.

Admiration: Look for positive words and expressions.

- 'good, solid, comfortable': suggests he was successful in life
- 'worked his way': suggests he was hard-working
- 'joined the army': showed bravery and initiative.

Sympathy: Look for negative words and expressions such as 'felt unloved' (sounds lonely and sad); 'tragedy', 'mother died young' (suggests a sense of loss); 'cancer' (a particularly frightening disease).

Hints and Tips

In a word choice question, always remember to *quote*.

Find four quotations for a 4 mark answer and comment on each one separately.

Answer

We admire the fact that Schulz 'joined the army' during the Second World War as this shows bravery and initiative. 'Worked his way through art school' is admirable as it suggests he was conscientious. We feel sympathetic towards him as we are told that he 'felt unloved' by everyone other than his parents, implying that he was sad and lonely. The fact that 'his mother died young' of cancer, a particularly frightening disease, suggests a deep sense of loss which increases the reader's sympathy. (4 marks)

Question

11 In this passage the writer's main purpose is to explain why the Peanuts cartoon strip has been so successful.

By referring closely to the text, clearly explain which of his reasons you find the most convincing.

(4 marks) E

The final question in an Intermediate 2 Close Reading paper is an Evaluation question which often asks you to look back over the whole passage, or at least a substantial section of it.

This question is often poorly answered, partly because a lengthier explanation is required and partly, no doubt, because some candidates run out of time and rush their answers at the end.

First, you need to be clear about the reasons for the cartoon's success. Most of the relevant points can be found between lines 32 and 43 and could be summarised as follows:

- Like real people, the characters in the stories want to be loved, and that theme appeals to every reader.
- The drawings and text are simple and easy to follow but at the same time they contain deeper thoughts.
- The comic strips are amusing and the humour is sometimes quite hard-hitting, even sarcastic.
- The characters are children but they behave in grown-up ways.
- Charles Schulz drew on his own experiences of life when creating his characters and story lines.

Explaining these reasons would obviously produce quite a substantial answer. However, simply accounting for the popularity of the comic strip is not exactly what the question is asking. It says 'clearly explain which of his reasons you find the most convincing'.

This means that as well as summarising the reasons, you have to express a view on how persuasive these reasons are – the 'evaluation' bit. Don't be frightened to say things like 'I felt that such and such was convincing'.

Again, the best way of understanding what is required is to look at a couple of candidates' attempts.

Answers

(i) Charles Schulz's cartoons were so successful because they are funny and the characters behave like adults. The drawings are simple and 'the characters speak of a universal desire to be loved'. Jean Schulz, the wife of the cartoonist, attributed the success of the cartoon to 'how much of himself Schulz put into it'. The cartoonist was not surprised that his strip caught on in such a big way because he had been planning for it to be successful ever since he was six years old. I found these reasons for the success of the Peanuts cartoon strip very convincing.

(ii) The writer gives various reasons for the popularity of the Peanuts comic strip. One that I found convincing was that the strip's success came from the fact that the drawings and text were 'funny, poignant' and 'deceptively simple' – in other words, they were easy to follow and amusing, yet they dealt with deeper human emotions that everyone can relate to, such as the longing to be loved. I felt that even though these emotions are experienced by adults they are easier to relate to in the comic strip because the characters are children ('unusually mature kids'). However, I was less convinced by the argument that the cartoon was popular because of 'how much of himself Schulz put into it' because I felt that the stories would still be just as entertaining or moving even if they had not actually happened to him.

(i)	This is well-expressed and includes detail – but how relevant is it? The candidate summarises reasons for the cartoon's popularity, but then goes on to mention other points that add nothing to the answer. The last sentence of the answer refers to the question but simply says that the candidate found *all* the reasons convincing. There is no 'evaluation' of these reasons.	2 marks
(ii)	This answer also summarises some reasons for the strip's popularity but is of better quality as it goes on to make clear *why* the candidate found them convincing. The writer shows enough confidence to disagree with one of the points made in the passage. (Whether or not the examiner shares this opinion does not matter.) This is not a perfect answer, but it is a very good one to have been produced under exam conditions.	4 marks

PART 2

Paper 2: Critical Essay

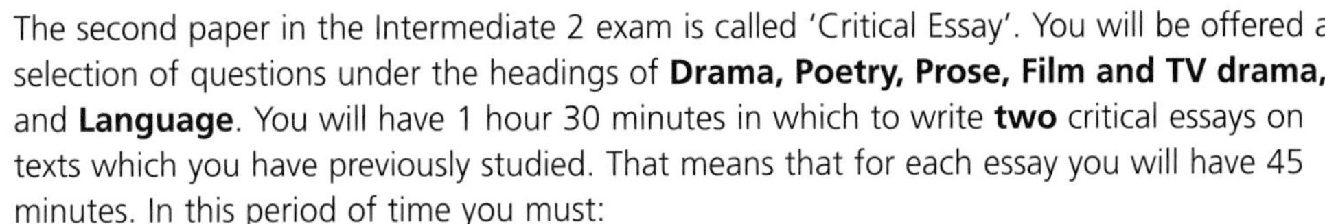

The second paper in the Intermediate 2 exam is called 'Critical Essay'. You will be offered a selection of questions under the headings of **Drama, Poetry, Prose, Film and TV drama,** and **Language**. You will have 1 hour 30 minutes in which to write **two** critical essays on texts which you have previously studied. That means that for each essay you will have 45 minutes. In this period of time you must:

- select a question
- plan your answer
- write the essay
- check over your essay for errors.

What are examiners looking for in the critical essay?

The critical essay will be marked under five criteria:

Relevance: your essay must provide a line of argument which is relevant to the question you choose.

Understanding: you must show understanding of key elements and central concerns of the text, and knowledge of significant details.

Analysis: you must explain the ways in which aspects of structure, style and language contribute to the meaning, effect or impact of your text. You should be able to use appropriate critical terminology in your explanations.

Evaluation: you must comment on how effective the writer has been, using appropriate detail and relevant evidence in your essay.

Expression: technically, your writing should be accurate in terms of grammar, spelling and punctuation. Your style should be appropriately formal.

I'm not sure if I can write without *any* mistakes. Does that mean I am sure to fail?

Intermediate 2 asks that your expression should be 'sufficiently' accurate. This is quite a vague term, but it means that you may make a few errors without being in danger of failing.

What is 'appropriate critical terminology'?

This rather alarming expression basically just means terms such as simile, metaphor, personification and so on. You will have been taught these by your teacher or tutor, so you must be sure to make use of such terms in your essay. A list of the ones you should know is to be found at the end of this book (pages 129–130).

What does 'critical' mean? Do I have to include some criticisms and things I *don't* like in my essay?

'Critical' in this context refers to analysing and evaluating a text, not making negative comments. You should always aim to be **positive** in your evaluation.

What will the questions be like?

It is never possible to predict exactly what will be in the questions, since there may be changes from one year to another. However, the plan for the layout from 2006 onwards is as follows:

Each section will begin with a box containing a list of 'relevant features' which you might include in your discussion. For example, in the case of the prose section, the box contains the following introduction:

> Answers to questions in this section should refer to the text and to such relevant features as: characterisation, key scene(s), structure, climax, theme, plot, conflict, setting . . .

In the case of drama, the box will include drama specific terms such as 'key scenes' and 'soliloquy', as well as more general ones, such as 'theme'. In the case of poetry, the list will include 'word choice', 'tone' and 'imagery' among others. The lists in the boxes are there as a reminder to discuss your text critically, and not simply retell it. You should **not** structure your essay around the topics, for example by dividing up your essay into sections with subheadings.

Each section will contain **three** questions.

Each question will contain **two** sentences.

The example on page 61 is taken from the Specimen Critical Essay paper for examinations in and after 2006 and shows how the questions will be laid out in the exam booklet.

- The **first sentence** will begin with the word 'choose'. It will ask you firstly to 'choose' an example of a **genre** (poem, play, novel, etc.) and then it will narrow your choice by adding a **description** such as 'which deals with family life'. You should refer directly to this sentence in your introduction:

  'A novel which deals with family life is… .'

- The **second sentence** is the key to the question, and will instruct you on what you must *do* in your essay; for example: 'Show how the relationships within the family affect the events and outcome of the story.' This sentence provides **the topic which you must focus on**. You should refer to this sentence both in your introduction and frequently throughout your essay, to show that you have maintained this focus. It is vitally important that you do this so that you satisfy the criterion of relevance.

SECTION B—PROSE

Answers to questions in this section should refer to the text and to such relevant features as: characterisation, setting, language, key incident(s), climax/turning point, plot, structure, narrative technique, theme, ideas, description . . .

4. Choose one or more prose works (novel, short story(ies), essay(s), journalism) which deal(s) with family or community life.

   Show how differing points of view in the family or community are developed in the work(s) you have chosen, and how they have influenced your thinking.

5. Choose a novel or short story in which there is an obvious climax or turning point.

   Show how the writer leads up to this turning point or climax, and say what its significance is for the rest of the story.

6. Choose a prose work of fiction or non-fiction which creates a sense of time and place.

   Show how the sense of time and place is created and evaluate its importance in your appreciation of the main concerns of the prose work.

SECTION C—POETRY

Answers to questions in this section should refer to the text and to such relevant features as: word choice, tone, imagery, structure, content, rhythm, theme, sound, ideas . . .

7. Choose a poem which deals with a happy experience.

   Briefly describe the experience and show how the poet has communicated the feelings of happiness by the use of various poetic techniques.

8. Choose a poem which increased your understanding of any aspect of life in the modern world.

   State what aspect of life in the modern world the poem illustrates and go on to show how the poem, both by its content and by its style, increased your understanding.

9. Choose a poem which deals with a particular time of year.

   Show how the poet, by her or his choice of content and skilful use of techniques, helps you to appreciate the positive or negative aspects of the time of year described.

Note: You are *not* allowed to take any notes or texts into the exam room with you.

Chapter 5

WRITING A CRITICAL ESSAY ON POETRY

Poetry is a popular choice for the Critical Essay, and if you choose a poem of high quality which you genuinely engage with you are likely to gain a good mark.

The methods explained here can be applied to any poem, but a very well-known one has been chosen as an example: 'Dulce et Decorum Est' by the First World War poet Wilfred Owen. You may well have read this poem in class.

© Imperial War Museum

Wilfred Owen is the best-known poet of the First World War. He died in action in France on 4 November 1918 at the age of only 25. News of his death reached his family a week later on 11 November – the day when Britain was celebrating the end of the war.

Much of the advice given here will also be useful for approaching Textual Analysis exercises. These involve reading a previously unseen poem and answering questions on it. (While this exercise doesn't form part of the Intermediate 2 examination, it is one of the internal assessments that you have to pass before proceeding to the final exam).

Reading the poem: identifying the main points

On first reading you should simply aim to form a general impression of what the poem is about – the **content** rather than the style. To help with this, try to describe in one phrase or sentence what each section or verse of the poem deals with.

Then, in note form, summarise the main points made in each section.

Dulce et Decorum Est

SECTION ONE (lines 1–8) *Description of the soldiers marching back to base*

Bent double, like old beggars under sacks,
Knock-kneed, coughing like hags, we cursed through sludge,
Till on the haunting flares we turned our backs
And towards our distant rest began to trudge.
Men marched asleep. Many had lost their boots
But limped on, blood-shod. All went lame; all blind;
Drunk with fatigue; deaf even to the hoots
Of tired, outstripped Five-Nines that dropped behind.

poor physical condition

lack of awareness of what is going on around them

SECTION TWO (lines 9–14) *Description of the gas attack*

Gas! Gas! Quick, boys! – An ecstasy of fumbling,
Fitting the clumsy helmets just in time;
But someone still was yelling out and stumbling,
And flound'ring like a man in fire or lime …
Dim, through the misty panes and thick green light,
As under a green sea, I saw him drowning.

soldiers forced to react quickly

one man fails to fit his helmet in time

SECTION THREE (lines 15–16) *The poet's nightmares about the incident*

In all my dreams, before my helpless sight,
He plunges at me, guttering, choking, drowning.

he keeps seeing the dying man and is haunted by the fact that he could not help him

SECTION FOUR (lines 17–28) *Description of the suffering of one particular soldier, leading up to the 'moral' or message of the poem*

If in some smothering dreams you too could pace
Behind the wagon that we flung him in,
And watch the white eyes writhing in his face,
His hanging face, like a devil's sick of sin;
If you could hear, at every jolt, the blood
Come gargling from the froth-corrupted lungs,
Obscene as cancer, bitter as the cud
Of vile, incurable sores on innocent tongues,
My friend, you would not tell with such high zest
To children ardent for some desperate glory,
The old Lie; Dulce et Decorum est
Pro patria mori.

victim is brutally thrown into a wagon

emphasis on the horrific effects of the gas on the dying man

bitter attack on the 'patriots' who have sent young men out to die

What is said and how it's said

For convenience in note-making, a poem can be looked at in terms of **content**, **style** and **evaluation**.

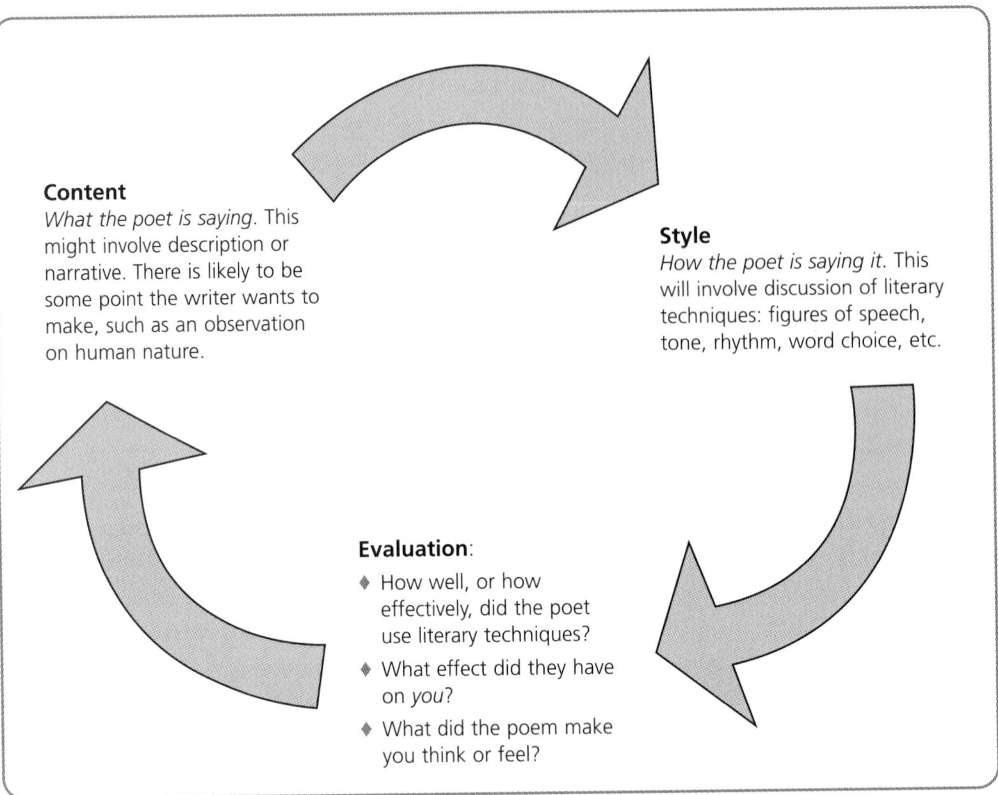

Content
What the poet is saying. This might involve description or narrative. There is likely to be some point the writer wants to make, such as an observation on human nature.
Style
How the poet is saying it. This will involve discussion of literary techniques: figures of speech, tone, rhythm, word choice, etc.
Evaluation:
♦ How well, or how effectively, did the poet use literary techniques?
♦ What effect did they have on *you*?
♦ What did the poem make you think or feel?

Making notes on the writer's style

Having identified the key points of the poem, you should now find examples of poetic techniques used to convey these points (**style**).

Perhaps the most straightforward to identify are figures of speech (simile/metaphor/alliteration, etc. see pages 129–130 for a list of definitions).

Equally, you should pick out examples of words and phrases that might not be figures of speech but which are particularly well-chosen or descriptive.

For Practice

Practise this skill by making notes on 'Dulce et Decorum Est' in the following format. One or two examples have been done for you already.

	Technique used	Example (quotation)
SECTION ONE (lines 1–8) Description of the soldiers marching back to base	*simile* *metaphor*	*'bent double, like old beggars under sacks'* *'drunk with fatigue'*
SECTION TWO (lines 9–14) Description of the gas attack	*Interesting word choice*	*floundering, fumbling, stumbling*
SECTION THREE (lines 15–16) The poet's nightmares about the incident		
SECTION FOUR (lines 17–28) Description of the suffering of one particular soldier, leading up to the 'moral' or message of the poem		

Evaluation

Simply 'sticking labels' on lines of a poem and identifying them as similes, metaphors, alliteration and so on is of course a rather mechanical approach to the appreciation of a poet's work! What you now have to do is to explain how the examples you have chosen actually work. You are frequently told to 'Comment on the effectiveness' of an expression. But what does this really mean?

This is where **evaluation** comes in. To explain *why* a poet's word choice or use of figures of speech is effective you have to use your imagination and think not so much about the meaning of a word but about its associations (or connotations). In other words, what picture does this word or expression bring into your mind?

Example

Take the simile in the opening line of the poem:

'Bent double, like old beggars under sacks'

Here, each soldier marching back to base is compared to an old beggar carrying his belongings over his shoulder in a sack.

- Think about the word 'beggar'. Make a list of the things you associate this word with.
- Why does Owen compare the soldiers to 'old' beggars when they are probably young recruits in their teens?

Example *continued* ➢

***Example** continued*

Asking questions like these helps you to understand the implications of the comparison and enables you to comment on it in a more detailed way:

> This was an effective comparison because it suggests that the soldiers are dirty, badly-nourished and laden down with the heavy burden of the equipment they are carrying. The use of the word 'old' reminds us that although these soldiers are probably young recruits, the strain of the war has taken its toll on them and has prematurely aged them.

For Practice

Choose some of the examples of the poet's word choice and use of figures of speech that you quoted in the table on the previous page.

In each case, write a comment on why you thought the language was used effectively.

It's a good idea to practise this skill, especially if you are intending to apply the lessons of this chapter to another poem you've been studying.

However, if you're in a hurry, look ahead to pages 75–76 where you will find a detailed set of notes analysing the style of 'Dulce et Decorum Est'.

Writing a critical essay

You should now have quite a detailed set of notes on the poem. But writing an essay involves more than just learning and rewriting your notes – as you may already have found to your cost!

Reading the question

The basic point to grasp here is that you are never going to be asked simply to 'write an essay on a poem'. Instead you are asked to answer a particular question on the poem. The secret of writing a good critical essay is to present your knowledge of the text in a way that fits the question set. The same ideas can be used in different essays but each time they must be presented in a way that fits the specific question.

At the top of this section of the paper there will be a box with a list of 'relevant features' you might include in your discussion:

> Answers to questions in this section should refer to the text and to such relevant features as: word choice, tone, imagery, structure, content, rhythm, theme, sound, ideas . . .

Look at this past paper question.

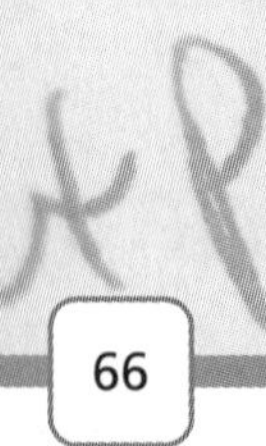

Question

Choose a poem where the poet starts off by describing an everyday happening or incident and then goes on to make a deeper or more serious point about human nature by the end of the poem.

Briefly describe the starting point of the poem and state what you think is the serious point made by the end. Now go on to show how the poet's use of poetic techniques deepens your understanding of the poem.

Reading the question carefully will provide you with many clues about how to approach the essay.

- 'Dulce et Decorum Est' starts by describing what was an everyday incident in the First World War and ends by making a serious point. It therefore fits the question well.
- The question tells you what the structure of the essay should be like. You are asked to describe 'briefly' how the poem starts and then to explain the serious point made by the end. The rest of the essay should focus on the poet's **techniques**.
- Various topics (word choice, tone, imagery, structure, content, rhythm, theme, sound, ideas, etc.) are suggested at the start of the Poetry section of the exam paper. If you do not want to write about (for example) structure, but wish to talk about imagery (figures of speech) then this is all right. In practice, though, any essay on poetry is likely to choose word choice as one of the main techniques. After all, a poem is made up of words!
- The question asks you to 'show how the poet's use of poetic techniques deepens your understanding of the poem'. It is not enough to identify the techniques used; you must go on to explain how they work and why they are effective in adding to your understanding of what the poem is about.
- The instructions also say that you should *refer to the text*. This means that detailed examples and quotations must be included.

All the above advice comes straight from the question, but many students do not bother to read the question properly and simply pour out all their memorised notes.

The remainder of this section shows you how to plan and write an essay answer to this question.

Getting off to the right start: the introductory paragraph

You should always focus on the question as early as possible in your essay – and that means right from the opening sentence. An experienced examiner can quickly tell whether a student is going to answer the question directly or whether he or she is simply going to repeat prepared material.

How would you rate each of the following as opening paragraphs?

Answers

1 Wilfred Owen is one of the most famous poets of the First World War. He died in action in France in November 1918 at the age of only 25.

2 'Dulce et Decorum Est' describes the conditions suffered by soldiers marching back to base during the First World War. The poet uses a simile: 'Bent double, like old beggars under sacks'.

3 'Dulce et Decorum Est' by Wilfred Owen is a poem which starts off by describing an everyday incident and then goes on to make a more serious point about human nature.

The first example takes a biographical approach. It does not refer to the poem or to the question.	✗
The second example refers to the poem but not to the question. The introduction should take a general approach and should not start to discuss language techniques or give quotations.	✗
The third example immediately connects the chosen poem to the words of the question.	✓

Giving a short account

Next, the question asks you to:

Briefly describe the starting point of the poem and state what you think is the serious point made by the end.

This part of the question relates to the content of the poem rather than its style. The notes summarising the main points of the poem on page 63 could be used here. Note that you are asked to do this *briefly*. There is no need to quote at this stage, and you should not start discussing language techniques in this paragraph.

For Practice

Write a paragraph of about 6–8 lines answering this part of the question.

Examining the text in more detail

The main body of the essay (about 75% of it) will be concerned with the next part of the question:

Now go on to show how the poet's use of poetic techniques deepens your understanding of the poem.

At this point you should again refer to the words of the question. Begin with a general topic sentence rather than a detailed point.

How would your rate each of the following as an opening sentence for the part of the essay dealing with poetic techniques?

Answers

1 Owen uses the metaphor 'drunk with fatigue' to compare the effects of tiredness to the effects of alcohol.

2 'Coughing like hags', 'like old beggars under sacks' and 'drunk with fatigue' are some examples of the similes and metaphors that Wilfred Owen uses.

3 One of the main techniques which Owen used to deepen my understanding of the poem was imagery.

1	This sentence goes straight to a detailed example without a reference to the question.	✗
2	Too many examples are given in one sentence. Again, there has been no introductory topic sentence.	✗
3	This is a general introductory point that makes it clear what the rest of the paragraph is going to discuss and uses words from the question.	✓

The next stage is to expand the general introductory point in detail, by providing examples and quotations.

Using quotations properly

There may have been times when you wrote an essay and used plenty of quotations, but still did not receive a very good mark. Simply using quotations is not enough – you have to use them properly.

The basic rule is: ***quotations should be used to back up a point.***

Here are some extracts from students' essays. How well would you say they have employed quotations?

Answers

1 The poet describes how the soldiers had difficulty fitting their clumsy helmets just in time before the gas attack: "Fitting the clumsy helmet just in time."

2 In 'Dulce et Decorum Est' Wilfred Owen describes the poor condition of the soldiers marching back to base:

"Bent double, like old beggars, under sacks,
Knock-kneed, coughing like hags, we cursed through sludge
Till on the haunting flares we turned our backs
And towards our distant rest began to trudge.
Men marched asleep. Many had lost their boots,
But limped on, blood-shod.'

In the next verse, he describes how one man didn't manage to fit his gas helmet in time.

3 In verse one of the poem, Owen uses similes to describe the soldiers. 'Bent double, like old beggars under sacks', 'Coughing like hags'. He also uses a metaphor: 'men marched asleep.' 'Drunk with fatigue' is another example of a metaphor.

4 There is a contrast between the pace of verse one and verse two. In the first verse, words like 'trudge', 'distant' and 'limped on' suggest that the march back to base was painfully slow. In verse two, however, the pace speeds up:

'Gas! Gas! Quick, boys!'

Here, there is a series of single words separated by exclamation marks which conveys a sense of urgency. Although the soldiers are desperately tired, they must respond quickly or the gas will affect their lungs.

5 The writer uses quotes to describe how tired the soldiers are, e.g. 'towards our distant rest began to trudge'. The writer also uses the quote 'drunk with fatigue'. These quotes show how tired the soldiers were.

1	The quotation adds nothing here. It simply repeats what has just been said, in exactly the same words.	✗
2	The quotation is far too long and is not followed up by any detailed comment.	✗
3	The student identifies figures of speech and quotes examples. However, too many separate examples are listed without any detailed comments.	✗
4	This extract uses quotations well. They back up the point made and they are followed by a detailed comment on why they are effective.	✓
5	Extracts from a text should not be referred to as 'quotes'. Writers do not write 'quotes' – *you* are quoting the writer!	✗

The 'statement – quotation – comment' pattern

The fourth answer on the previous page is a good example of how to use quotations properly.

Opening sentence makes a general statement (topic sentence)

Linking word

There is a contrast between the pace of verse one and verse two. In the first verse, words like 'trudge', 'distant' and 'limped on' suggest that the march back to base was painfully slow. In verse two, **however**, the pace speeds up:

'Gas! Gas! Quick, boys!'

Here, there is a series of single words separated by exclamation marks which conveys a sense of urgency. Although the soldiers are desperately tired, they must respond quickly or the gas will affect their lungs.

Quotations are followed by comment on their effectiveness

Second example, again followed by detailed comment

For Practice

Practise writing a paragraph like this by filling in the gaps with some of the examples of figures of speech and effective word choice that you included in your table on page 65.

Wilfred Owen uses a number of different figures of speech to describe the physical and mental suffering of the soldiers marching back to base. For example … This [simile/metaphor/word choice, etc.] is effective because … A similar example is … Here the poet describes how …

Now write a similar paragraph of your own, based on the same pattern:

- Begin with a general statement.
- Quote an example.
- Comment on why the example is effective.

Writing the essay (at last!)

All the material covered in this chapter can now be reworked into an essay answer.

You should now have:

- an understanding of the main points of 'Dulce et Decorum Est'
- an appreciation of the poetic techniques used
- a knowledge of how to back up points with quotations and detailed comments
- a knowledge of how an essay should be structured: reference to the question; introductory paragraph, short account; detailed analysis of the poet's techniques.

For Practice

At this stage, you should go over everything in this chapter again and attempt to write an essay in answer to the past paper question on page 67.

If you are studying this book as part of your last-minute revision, you could try putting the notes aside and writing the essay in the 45 minute time limit that you'll have in the examination.

You can then compare this with the sample essay which follows on page 73. Virtually all the points made in the essay are based on the material contained in this chapter, to show you how you can restructure your notes into the appropriate essay format.

Checking it over

You've written the essay – but there's still one final thing to do: **Check it over**!

Too many essays are marked down because they are full of errors of punctuation, spelling and style which could have been eliminated if the essay had been proof-read.

In Chapter 10 'Technical Accuracy' (pages 125–128) you will find a useful checklist of some of the most common faults to avoid.

Sample Critical Essay on 'Dulce et Decorum Est'

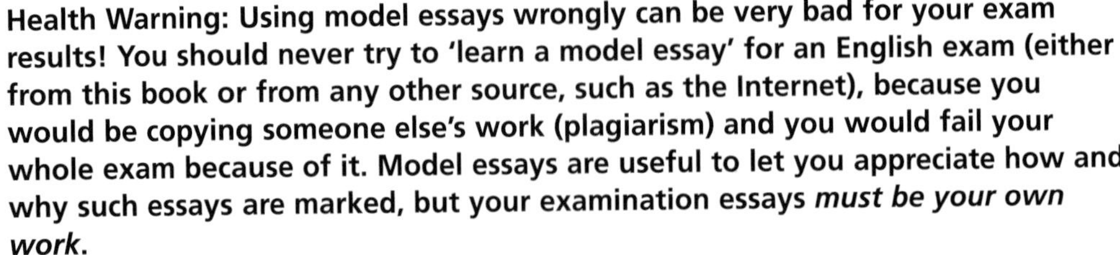

Health Warning: Using model essays wrongly can be very bad for your exam results! You should never try to 'learn a model essay' for an English exam (either from this book or from any other source, such as the Internet), because you would be copying someone else's work (plagiarism) and you would fail your whole exam because of it. Model essays are useful to let you appreciate how and why such essays are marked, but your examination essays *must be your own work*.

The following is an example of an essay that would fulfil all the criteria of Intermediate 2. Do *not* try to learn it off by heart! However, look carefully at how it is structured, how it has an introduction and conclusion and how quotations are worked into the paragraph structure.

Question

Choose a poem where the poet starts off by describing an everyday happening or incident and then goes on to make a deeper or more serious point about human nature by the end of the poem.

Briefly describe the starting point of the poem and state what you think is the serious point made by the end. Now go on to show how the poet's use of poetic techniques deepens your understanding of the poem.

(You should also remember the general instruction that applies to all questions in the Poetry section of the paper: answers to questions in this section should refer to the text and to such relevant features as: word choice, tone, imagery, structure, content, rhythm, theme, sound, ideas . . .)

Answer

'Dulce et Decorum Est' by Wilfred Owen is a poem which starts off by describing an everyday incident and then goes on to make a deeper point about human nature.

Opening paragraph uses words from the question

The poem begins by depicting a common event during the First World War: exhausted soldiers returning to base find themselves subjected to a sudden gas attack and are forced to respond quickly. Most of the poem focuses on the sufferings of one soldier who does not manage to fit his gas mask in time. The horror of his death, says Owen, shows that the notion that it is a 'sweet and fitting thing to die for one's country' is completely untrue.

Short account

One of the poetic techniques used by Owen to deepen the reader's understanding of the poem is imagery. For example, the soldiers are described as 'Bent double, like old beggars under sacks'. This simile emphasises the weight of the heavy equipment they are carrying and suggests how dirty, unhealthy and badly-nourished the soldiers are. I found it interesting that Owen compared these young recruits to 'old' beggars: it is as if they have been prematurely aged by their experience of war. Another image which helps to convey the poor condition of the soldiers is the metaphor 'drunk with fatigue'. Here the mental effects of extreme tiredness, such as lack of co-ordination and a lack of awareness of surroundings, are compared to the effects of alcohol.

Topic sentence, referring to words from the question

Quotation

Comment

Personal response

Further quotation/ comment

In addition to making such comparisons, Owen's effective word choice strengthens the impact of the poem on the reader. At the start, he uses the word 'trudged' to describe the soldiers' manner of marching – a slow, heavy-sounding word which reflects how weary they are and how each

Linking expression

New topic introduced

Answer *continued* ➢

Answer continued

step is an effort. By contrast, the second verse begins with a series of short monosyllabic words – 'Gas! Gas! Quick, boys!' – reflecting the change of pace and creating a sense of urgency, reinforced by the use of exclamation marks. Present participles such as 'fumbling', 'stumbling' and 'flound'ring' indicate that the soldiers have difficulty fitting their gas masks and create an impression of helplessness.

Further back-up examples

In the fourth section Wilfred Owen chooses words that emphasise the horrific suffering of the soldier who did not manage to fit his mask in time. All his agony is concentrated in 'white eyes writhing in his face'. 'Writhing' makes the reader imagine the man twisting and squirming in pain, an effect which is made still stronger by the use of alliteration. The poet's word choice reminds us that the horror of watching the victim suffer involves all the human senses, not only sight but also sound and taste. This can be seen, for example, in the unpleasant connotations of 'gargling from the froth-corrupted lungs' or in the simile 'bitter as the cud', an expression which draws on an old superstition once told to children that lying could cause sores in the mouth. As well as all this physical pain, there is an emotional aspect to his suffering: we are told that his comrades 'flung' him into a wagon. The word suggests a violent action and shows there was no time for compassion or ceremony.

Discussion of word choice in verse four

However, of all the poetic techniques used in the poem, perhaps the most effective is the tone of irony at the end. The serious point of the poem is only spelt out in the last four lines, when the reader realises why the death of the soldier has been described in such detail. Throughout the poem Owen has employed the first person (I and we) to show that he had personally experienced this event. He then uses the second person 'you' to address his imagined readers, the stay-at-home patriots who encouraged young men (so young that they are called 'children') to go to war in the belief that dying for their country would be a glorious experience. If such people had ever seen what it was like to die in war, says Owen, they would realise that it was anything but glorious. The poet ironically addresses these readers as 'my friend', emphasising his bitter anger towards them. At the end of the poem we realise that the title, too, was ironic. Using part of the Latin poet's famous saying 'Dulce et decorum est pro patria mori' as a title might have led the reader to expect a rousing patriotic message, whereas the poet's intention is quite the opposite.

Linking word indicates change to different topic

Explanation of the last verse and the technique of irony

Thus, in 'Dulce et Decorum Est' Wilfred Owen starts by describing an everyday happening in the First World War and goes on to present a serious message about how young men had been misled into sacrificing their lives in a meaningless slaughter. I felt that my understanding of this message had been deepened by the poet's use of imagery, effective word choice and irony.

Concluding paragraph sums up main points and refers back to the question again

(795 words)

Notes on 'Dulce et Decorum Est'

Section One (lines 1–8): Description of the soldiers marching back to base

Physical suffering of the soldiers

- 'Bent double': weighed down by their heavy equipment.
- 'like old beggars under sacks': a **simile** suggesting how dirty, unhealthy and badly-fed the soldiers are. Though young men, they are described as 'old', showing how the war has prematurely aged them.
- 'coughing like hags': another **simile**. A hag is an elderly and unattractive woman; the simile reinforces the idea of the soldiers being aged and degraded by their experiences.
- 'trudge': slow, heavy-sounding word, reflecting how weary they are and how each step is an effort.
- 'blood-shod': some of the soldiers have lost their boots and their feet are encrusted with blood and the mud of the trenches.
- Note the use of 'we': first person plural emphasises that Owen had experienced these conditions personally.

Mental effects

- 'Drunk with fatigue': a **metaphor** comparing the mental effects of tiredness with the effects of alcohol, e.g. lack of coordination, lack of awareness of surroundings, etc.
- 'blind / deaf': the soldiers are not literally blind or deaf; these lines refer again to the debilitating effects of exhaustion which dulls their senses and makes them slow to react to the gas shells.

Section Two (lines 9–14): Description of the gas attack

- 'Gas! Gas! Quick, boys!': note the **change of pace** here. The slow laborious pace of the march was reflected in the long sentences of verse one; here, short words and exclamation marks are used to stress the sense of urgency.
- 'ecstasy': normally used to refer to a state of great excitement, the word *ecstasy* is also used as a medical term to refer to a highly nervous state in which the mind is preoccupied with one idea alone.
- 'fumbling / fitting / stumbling / flound'ring': grammatically, these words are known as **present participles** (verb form ending in–*ing*). They denote an ongoing state or condition rather than a one-off action, indicating that the process of trying to fit the gas masks continued for some time. Note, too, that most of these words suggest the idea of helplessness, of actions attempted but not quite completed.
- 'flound'ring like a man in fire or lime': in this **simile** the helplessness and agony of being caught in a gas attack is compared to dying in a fire or in lime (a chemical that burns the skin).
- 'As under a green sea': the experience is also compared to drowning. The poet combines contrasting elements – fire and water – which would normally cancel each other out, as if to suggest that dying in a gas attack is so horrific that it is like burning and drowning simultaneously.
- The use of **ellipsis** (three dots) implies that this process went on for some time.

Section Three (lines 15–16): The poet's nightmares about the incident

The structure and rhyme scheme of the first and second verses are similar, except for the fact that these two lines are laid out separately. This is the only part of the poem that is not taking place in the war zone: the poet relives the experience again and again, and is particularly distressed by the fact that there is nothing he can do to help (expressed by the **transferred epithet** 'helpless sight'). Present participles are used again ('guttering', 'choking', 'drowning') to emphasise the suffering of the victim, a theme which is continued further in the last part of the poem.

Section Four (lines 17–28): Description of the suffering of the particular soldier, leading up to the 'moral' or message of the poem

- Owen now uses the second person 'you' to address the reader directly. The whole verse is structured as one sentence, leading up to a climax in the last four lines.
- The victim is violently 'flung' into a wagon: there is no time for compassion or ceremony.
- It is clear that the man is not yet dead: he cannot convey his suffering in words, but his agony is concentrated in his eyes, emphasised by the strong alliteration of 'watch the white eyes writhing in his face';
- The simile 'his hanging face, like a devil's sick of sin' implies that war is such an evil that Satan himself might turn against it in revulsion.
- The whole thrust of this verse is to stress the horror of having to watch this man suffer – a suffering that involves not only the sense of sight but also of sound and taste, as in 'gargling from the froth-corrupted lungs' and 'bitter as the cud'. The latter expression draws on an old superstitious belief once told to children that lying could cause sores in the mouth.
- Only in the last four lines does the reader grasp why Owen has described this incident with such force. *Dulce et decorum est pro patria mori* means, literally, 'It is a sweet and fitting thing to die for one's country'. Owen's aim is to undermine the title of the poem by showing that in real life, dying for your country is *not* a 'sweet and fitting thing'.
- There is bitter **irony** in the way that Owen addresses the stay-at-home patriots as 'my friend'. (Originally he had in mind Jessie Pope, who wrote patriotic recruiting poems urging young men to give their lives for their country.)

WRITING A CRITICAL ESSAY ON PROSE

The prose option in the Intermediate 2 Critical Essay paper offers the choice of writing about a short story, a novel or a work of non-fiction.

- A **novel** is a full-length work of fiction.
- **Short stories** are short works of fiction which are not published individually but in a collection. They may be of varying length – some are as much as 40 pages long.
- **Non-fiction** (factual writing) is a difficult option to choose, as the quality of writing is not always good even if the topic may be interesting.

A short story by a recognised author is a good choice for your Critical Essay as it is a manageable length to get to know and write about.

There are many good short story writers and many stories to choose from. The one that follows is by a contemporary Scottish writer, Bernard MacLaverty. It offers an intriguing **plot**; an interesting central **character** whose plight arouses our sympathy; a well-drawn **setting**; a clear **theme**; and striking use of **language** and **imagery**.

You will be asked to:

- work through various questions which will help you get to know and understand the story. (You should check your answers as you go along.)
- write an essay on one of the topics selected from past papers.
- read the specimen essay, which will give an indication of what you should be aiming at yourself.

Look at the title

Before you begin reading, consider MacLaverty's choice of title, 'Remote'. This title consists of a single adjective (describing word), which is quite unusual for a story title.

Question

What does the word 'remote' mean? Can it have more than one meaning? Write down a list of things which this adjective might be applied to. You could use a dictionary to help you. This may suggest some themes to you.

Check your answer on page 84.

Now read the story carefully. As you read, you might underline or annotate (note in the margin) any idea, word or phrase that strikes you as special in some way.

REMOTE

Bernard MacLaverty

Around about the end of each month she would write a letter, but because it was December she used an old Christmas card, which she found at the bottom of the biscuit tin among her pension books. She stood dressed in her outdoor clothes on tiptoe at the bedroom window waiting for the bird-watcher's Land Rover to come over the top of the hill two miles away. When she saw it she dashed, slamming the door after her and running in her stiff-legged fashion down the lane on to the road. Her aim was to be walking, breathing normally, when the Land Rover would indicate and stop in the middle of the one-track road.

'Can I give you a lift?'

'Aye.'

She walked round the front of the shuddering engine and climbed up to sit on the split seat. Mushroom-coloured foam bulged from its crack. More often than not she had to kick things aside to make room for her feet. It was not the lift she would have chosen but it was all there was. He shoved the wobbling stick through the gears and she had to shout – each month the same thing.

'Where are you for?'

'The far side.'

'I'm always lucky just to catch you.'

He was dressed like one of those hitch-hikers, green khaki jacket, cord trousers and laced-up mountain boots. His hair was long and unwashed and his beard divided into points like the teats of a goat.

'Are you going as far as the town this time?'

'Yes.'

'Will you drop me off?'

'Sure. Christmas shopping?'

'Aye, that'll be right.'

The road spun past, humping and squirming over peat bogs, the single track bulging at passing places – points which were marked by tall black and white posts to make them stand out against the landscape. Occasionally in the bog there were incisions, a black-brown colour, herring-boned with scars where peat had been cut.

'How's the birds doing?' she shouted.

'Fine. I've never had so many as this year.'

continued ➢

His accent was English and it surprised her that he had blackheads dotting his cheekbones and dirty hands.

'Twenty-two nesting pairs – so far.'

'That's nice.'

'Compared with sixteen last year.'

'What are they?'

He said what they were but she couldn't hear him properly. They joined the main road and were silent for a while. Then rounding a corner the bird-man suddenly applied the brakes. Two cars, facing in opposite directions, sat in the middle of the road, their drivers having a conversation. The bird-man muttered and steered round them, the Land Rover tilting as it mounted the verge.

'I'd like to see them try that in Birmingham.'

'Is that where you're from?'

He nodded.

'Why did you come to the island?'

'The birds.'

'Aye, I suppose there's not too many down there.'

He smiled and pointed to an open packet of Polo mints on the dashboard. She lifted them and saw that the top sweet was soiled, the relief letters almost black. She prised it out and gave it to him. The white one beneath she put in her mouth.

'Thanks,' she said.

'You born on the island?'

'City born and bred.' She snorted. 'I was lured here by a man forty-two years ago.'

'I never see him around.'

'I'm not surprised. He's dead this long time.' She cracked the ring of the mint between her teeth.

'I'm sorry.'

She chased the two crescents of mint around with her tongue.

'What did he do?'

'He drowned himself in the loch.'

'I'm sorry. I didn't mean that.'

'On Christmas Day. He was mad in the skull – away with the fairies.'

There was a long pause in which he said again that he was sorry. Then he said, 'What I meant was – what did he do for a living?'

'What does it matter now?'

The bird-man shook his head and concentrated on the road ahead.

'He was a shepherd,' she said. Then a little later, 'He was the driver. There should always be one in the house who can drive.'

He let her off at the centre of the village and she had to walk the steep hill to the Post Office. She breathed through her mouth and took a rest halfway up, holding on to a small railing. Distances grew with age.

Inside she passed over her pension book, got her money and bought a first-class stamp. She waited until she was outside before she took the letter from her bag. She licked the stamp, stuck it on the envelope and dropped it in the letter box. Walking down the hill was easier.

continued ➢

She went to the Co-op to buy sugar and tea and porridge. The shop was strung with skimpy tinselled decorations and the music they were playing was Christmas hits – 'Rudolf' and 'I Saw Mummy Kissing Santa Claus'. She only had a brief word with Elizabeth at the check-out because of the queue behind her. In the butcher's she bought herself a pork chop and some bacon. His bacon lasted longer than the packet stuff.

When she had her shopping finished she wondered what to do to pass the time. She could visit young Mary but if she did that she would have to talk. Not having enough things to say she felt awkward listening to the tick of the clock and the distant cries of sea birds. Chat was a thing you got out of the habit of when you were on your own all the time and, besides, Mary was shy. Instead she decided to buy a cup of tea in the café. And treat herself to an almond bun. She sat near the window where she could look out for the post van.

The café was warm and it, too, was decorated. Each time the door opened the hanging fronds of tinsel fluttered. On a tape somewhere carols were playing. Two children, sitting with their mother, were playing with a new toy car on the table-top. The cellophane wrapping had been discarded on the floor. They both imitated engine noises although only one of them was pushing it round the plates. The other sat waiting impatiently for his turn.

She looked away from them and stared into her tea. When they dredged him up on Boxing Day he had two car batteries tied to his wrists. He was nothing if not thorough. One of them had been taken from his own van parked by the loch shore and the thing had to be towed to the garage. If he had been a drinking man he could have been out getting drunk or fallen into bad company. But there was only the black depression. All that day the radio had been on to get rid of the dread.

When 'Silent Night' came on the tape and the children started to squabble over whose turn it was she did not wait to finish her tea but walked slowly to the edge of the village with her bag of shopping, now and again pausing to look over her shoulder. The scarlet of the post van caught her eye and she stood on the verge with her arm out. When she saw it was Stuart driving she smiled. He stopped the van and she ducked down to look in the window.

'Anything for me today?'

He leaned across to the basket of mail which occupied the passenger seat position and began to rummage through the bundles of letters and cards held together with elastic bands.

'This job would be all right if it wasn't for bloody Christmas.' He paused at her single letter. 'Aye, there's just one.'

'Oh good. You might as well run me up, seeing as you're going that way.'

He sighed and looked over his shoulder at a row of houses.

'Wait for me round the corner.'

She nodded and walked on ahead while he made some deliveries. The lay-by was out of sight of the houses and she set her bag down to wait. Stuart seemed to take a long time. She looked down at the loch in the growing dark. The geese were returning for the night, filling the air with their squawking. They sounded like a dance-hall full of people laughing and enjoying themselves, heard from a distance on the night wind.

The structure of the story

The story falls into four sections or 'movements'. (Did you notice the extra spacing between these sections?)

Question

Sum up very briefly what happens in each of the four sections.

Check your answer on page 84.

Filling in the gaps

Often, to appreciate a text fully, it is necessary to use your imagination and to work out some clues which the writer has given. It is not always possible to know the whole truth, and that is part of the appeal, as you become aware that you could interpret the clues in different ways.

The letter

MacLaverty does not tell us directly *why* she wrote the letter or *to whom* she wrote it or *what* she wrote in it. But look at the evidence.

- She writes a letter at the end of every month.
- This month she 'used an old Christmas card' she had been keeping in a biscuit tin. She does not use normal writing paper.
- She does not put the stamp on her letter in the post office, but takes it outside where no one can see her before stamping and posting it.
- When the postman has collected the mail, he has 'just one' letter for her.
- The postman 'sighed', as if this is a regular routine and he is rather exasperated.

Question

What do you think is being suggested?

Check your answer on page 84.

The truth about the past

MacLaverty does not tell us the truth about the woman's husband and his suicide directly. All the events are presented from *her* point of view, in *her* words and thoughts.

Questions

- Make notes on how her feelings towards her husband are conveyed.
- Make notes on how his suicide is conveyed.
- Pick out at least **three** quotations which suggest she resents what he did.
- Consider if she reveals any sense of loss or grief. Can you find any evidence of conflicting feelings?

Check your responses with the suggestions on pages 84–85.

Characterisation

MacLaverty presents the woman as being slightly mad, presumably because of the tragedy surrounding her husband's suicide. She has become 'remote' from reality, and leads a lonely, pathetic, isolated existence which is very moving to the reader.

Question

Collect the details (either in quotation or with brief references) which go to building up our picture of her. Look for information on her age, appearance, her acquaintances, how she relates to people, her pride, her isolation, her lack of a name.

Check your responses with the suggestions on pages 85–86.

Setting

Make notes on the setting of the story. The setting is an island. Why might this be significant? The woman's husband committed suicide on Christmas Day. The story takes place just before Christmas. How does the author's use of detail in describing decorations and carols contribute to the themes and atmosphere of the story? Consider how the author uses contrast as a technique.

Question

Collect quotations which illustrate the setting. Can you think of ways in which these details might be seen as symbolic?

Check your answers with the suggestions on page 86.

Language

Bernard MacLaverty is masterly in his use of imagery and description.

Questions

What do you think is the significance of the following quotations from the story? Try to think of the literal (actual) meaning and also how it might contain a metaphor.

- **a** *She climbed up to sit on the split seat. Mushroom-coloured foam bulged from its crack.*
- **b** *It was not the lift she would have chosen but it was all there was.*
- **c** *She cracked the ring of the mint between her teeth.*
- **d** *Distances grew with age.*
- **e** *Not having enough things to say she felt awkward listening to the tick of the clock and the distant cries of sea birds.*
- **f** *She looked down at the loch in the growing dark.*
- **g** *The geese … sounded like a dance-hall full of people laughing and enjoying themselves, heard from a distance on the night wind.*

Check your answers with the suggestions on pages 86–87.

Style

MacLaverty cleverly presents the story from the woman's point of view. At times we can hear her spoken voice in the language of the narrative, as though she is speaking to herself. Sometimes illogical comments are made, or cruel observations about people. There is also a sense of information being suppressed. In addition, her personality is conveyed through direct speech.

Questions

What do you think the following extracts from the story reveal about her?

- **a** *because it was December she used an old Christmas card*
- **b** *'Can I give you a lift?'*
  'Aye.'
- **c** *He was dressed like one of those hitch-hikers*
- **d** *Chat was a thing you got out of the habit of when you were on your own all the time and, besides, Mary was shy.*
- **e** *One of them had been taken from his own van parked by the loch shore and the thing had to be towed to the garage.*

Check your answers with the suggestions on page 87.

Answers

Look at the title (page 77)

'Remote' means:

- distant in time or space
- located far away
- aloof, or unfocused when referring to a person's manner.

The title suggests themes of isolation and loneliness.

The structure of the story (page 81)

1. The old woman writes a letter and then lies in wait for the bird-watcher so he can give her a lift to the village post office in his Land Rover.
2. In the Land Rover, she tells him that her husband was 'mad in the skull' and drowned himself in the loch on Christmas Day, many years ago.
3. She posts her letter and goes to the Co-op for her groceries.
4. She goes to the café to wait until the postman comes by. She asks if he has anything for her, and he gives her one letter. She then asks him for a lift home.

Filling in the gaps (page 81)

The letter

The clues suggest she is slightly mad, and is writing the letter to herself.

- An old Christmas card would not be suitable for writing a normal letter.
- She conceals the letter at the Post Office so that no one can see her stamping a letter with her own name and address on it.
- She seems to know there is a letter for her when she asks the postman.

She is so lonely that she is still eager to get her one letter as no one else writes to her. Although she is ridiculous, it is touching that someone should be so desperate that they write to themselves.

The truth about the past (page 82)

In some places she seems resentful of her husband.

- She seems to dislike the island to which he has brought her, being '*city born and bred*'. She '*snorted*' when the bird-man asked if she is a native of the island, suggesting she despises it.
- She says she was '*lured here by a man*'. '*Lured*' suggests she feels she was tricked or deceived in some way.
- Her husband worked as a shepherd, which seems a gentle occupation, but perhaps not appropriate for the husband of a city woman. He may have left her alone a lot.
- The fact that she does not name him seems strange and off-hand.

***Answers** continued* ➢

Answers continued

- She shows no emotion when telling of his death, which she does frankly and almost brutally, while the bird-man becomes tongue-tied and embarrassed at her confidences.
- Her tone in thinking of his suicide – 'He was nothing if not thorough' – sounds bitter.
- She even resents that he left his van in an awkward place: '*the thing had to be towed to a garage*'.
- She seems to wish he had just been a drunk or gone with bad company rather than suffering from '*the black depression*', and subjecting her to the strain of waiting with '*the radio to get rid of the dread*' when he went out and failed to return.

However, other evidence is less negative.

- She seems haunted by the horror of what he did: '*he had two car batteries tied to his wrists*'.
- Events, such as his van being left at the loch-side, are clearly still fresh in her mind.
- She has stayed on the island.
- While she is waiting for the postman at the end she '*looked down at the loch in the growing dark*'. This was the scene of his suicide.
- She says to the bird-watcher that '*he was the driver. There should always be one in the house who can drive*'. This is perhaps symbolic, suggesting that she feels lost without his guidance.

Characterisation (page 82)

- She is old, having a '*pension book*'; her romance took place '*forty-two years ago*'.
- She is physically ungainly: '*running in her stiff-legged fashion*' and beginning to suffer the weakness of old age, as she has to hold on to the railing on the hill up to the Post Office.
- She is proud – she pretends she just happens to be on the road when the bird-watcher drives past, and aims to be '*breathing normally*'. She says '*I'm always lucky to catch you*'.
- She seems to have no friends, talking only to strangers or casual acquaintances such as the girl at the Co-op check-out who has no time to talk.
- She seems unused to conversation, and her tone is quite rude: she just answers '*Aye*' to the offer of a lift. She realises, 'chat was a thing you got out of the habit of'.
- She seems to repel people. The bird-watcher drops her off as quickly as he can after the uncomfortable revelations, and the postman seems reluctant to take her and ashamed to be seen with her: '*Wait for me round the corner*'.
- No one seems to care much about her; she sits alone in the café and has to '*treat herself*' to a bun as no one else will.
- She seems to dislike people and sees the worst in them. She looks with distaste at the unwashed hair and blackheads of the bird-watcher, although he kindly gives her a lift.

***Answers** continued* ➢

Answers continued

- The fact that she is never named implies that no one knows her. Most pathetic of all is her writing of the letters which seem tied up with guilt and loss at the death of her husband.

Setting (page 82)

- The idea of an island is symbolic of isolation. The woman seems trapped on the island as if she is trapped by the tragedy of her past and perhaps by feelings of guilt.
- It is Christmas time (the anniversary of the suicide). The decorations such as the '*hanging fronds of tinsel*' and cheery carols '*I Saw Mummy Kissing Santa Claus*' seem to mock her feelings of desolation. The contrast between the idea of Christmas festivity and her own associations with the day is very poignant. In the café, although she can put up with the noisy children, she walks out when 'Silent Night' starts playing.
- The description of the birds which are all in '*nesting pairs*' emphasises her lonely state, as does the description of the happy noises the geese make when they come to the loch to roost.
- The '*one track road*' on which she lives seems to suggest her lonely existence, with only death at the end of it.
- The detailed description of the landscape is also interesting. '*The road spun past, humping and squirming*' can be seen as a metaphor of her life and its ups and downs, with 'squirming' suggestive of pain. The '*passing places – points which were marked by tall black and white posts to make them stand out*' suggests landmarks in her otherwise dull life, such as her arrival in the island and her husband's death. The peat bog is '*herring-boned with scars*' where it has been cut. This is a powerful image, personifying the peat as if it has been injured. It makes us think of what she has suffered. The scars are like her trauma.

Language (page 83)

a As well as providing realistic detail of the interior of a beat-up old Land Rover, there is a suggestion of symbolism. The dirty-coloured foam rubber bursting out is like the unpleasant details erupting out of her mind.

b This quotation seems to stand for everything in the woman's life. It is full of pathos.

c This action comes after she says of her husband, '*He's dead this long time*'. It seems symbolic of the wedding ring and the marriage breaking up.

d This sums up her situation, and recalls the title of the story. Literally, it describes how much harder it is climbing the hill to the Post Office. Metaphorically, as she gets older, she becomes more remote from other people and from reality.

e This emphasises her loneliness, and reveals that the person she might call on is not really a friend. Her inability to communicate is conveyed, and the passing of time, in a seemingly wasted life, is symbolised by the '*tick of the clock*'. The '*cries of sea birds*' might reflect feelings in her own heart, expressing her deep unhappiness.

Answers continued ➢

Answers continued

f This emphasises how she has been unable to get on with her life after her husband's suicide. She is still obsessed with the loch where he drowned himself. The *'growing dark'* seems to symbolise her own life moving towards despair and death.

g This is a very effective simile, the lively geese evoking a scene of happy, cheerful people which contrasts with her own forlorn, lonely situation, summed up with the chill image of *'the night wind'* at *'a distance'*.

Style (page 83)

a This shows a lack of logical thought. It seems like the reasoning of a slightly crazy person, as a normal person would not use an old Christmas card to write a letter.

b Her response seems rude and abrupt, without the addition of a 'thank you'. Her lack of social graces suggests that people will be unlikely to like her or to pity her and so her loneliness will continue.

c The tone of disgust expressed in *'one of those'* suggests she would have nothing to do with such a person. There is also a lack of logic and self-awareness here, since she, herself, has just hitched a lift.

d Firstly she admits the truth about herself. However, she then makes an excuse, blaming someone else. We suspect that Mary, whoever she is, may not enjoy the woman's company either.

e Her tone of annoyance, in calling her husband's van 'the thing', seems to reflect her feelings about the husband himself. She resents what he has done and the 'dread' of waiting he has put her through the day he disappeared.

Writing the critical essay

You have now explored the story very thoroughly. You should have enough knowledge to tackle a number of questions.

Choose **one** of the following questions and write an essay on the story 'Remote' by Bernard MacLaverty.

> Answers to questions in this section should refer to the text and to such relevant features as: characterisation, setting, language, key incident(s), climax/turning point, plot, structure, narrative technique, theme, ideas, description . . .

Question

1 Choose a character from a novel or short story who seems to you to be unfortunate in life, or for whom the ending is unhappy.

Show how much of the character's misfortune you feel is caused by his or her own personality and how much by other circumstances in the short story or novel.

Hints and Tips

You are not simply being asked to describe an unhappy character. You are being asked to analyse the reason for the character being unhappy. In 'Remote', you must consider how far the woman seems to be responsible for her own unhappiness, or how far it is due to other circumstances, such as being uprooted from the city, or her husband's depression. If you suggest her unhappiness is due to a combination of factors you are likely to be on the right lines.

Question

2 Choose a prose work of fiction or non-fiction in which the setting is important.

Show how the setting in time and/or place contributes to your enjoyment of the work.

Hints and Tips

'Enjoyment' may be understood quite loosely here. It might seem strange to talk of 'enjoying' such a dark tale, but you could show how the setting aids your appreciation and understanding, so that reading the story becomes satisfying.

Question

3 Choose a novel or short story which deals with a powerful human emotion, for example love, shame, hatred, fear, embarrassment, despair, joy, or any other strong emotion.

Show how the emotion you have chosen affects one, or more than one, of the characters, and go on to show how it affects the course of the story.

Hints and **Tips**

The strong emotion might be loneliness, but you could also discuss the sense of guilt which the woman seems to show. Don't forget the second part of the question: how the emotion affects the course of the story. Show how loneliness drives the plot, with the basic structure involving her sending a letter to herself and collecting it from the postman. Loneliness dominates the way she behaves, speaks and thinks. There are also flashbacks which explain her loneliness and isolation.

Question

4 Choose a novel or short story where one of the main characters is female.

Show how the character's contribution to the content and outcome is important in the story as a whole.

Hints and **Tips**

Be sure to avoid just retelling the story if you choose this question. You could focus on the theme of loneliness and show how it is presented in the characterisation of the woman. 'Outcome' does not mean just the ending. In this story, the 'outcome' is the woman waiting alone in the darkening night for the postman to give her a lift. This symbolises her lonely old age stretching before her, a situation which is due to her own character and the tragic events in her life.

Question

5 Choose a work of fiction or non-fiction which deals with a serious aspect of life.

State what this serious aspect is and go on to show how your understanding of it was deepened by your reading of the work.

Hints and Tips

You could choose suicide as the 'serious aspect of life'. You can then consider the effect of the husband's suicide on the woman, and look at how reasons for the suicide are hinted at throughout the story.

Sample critical essay

Health Warning: Using model essays wrongly can be very bad for your exam results! You should never try to 'learn a model essay' for an English exam (either from this book or from any other source, such as the Internet), because you would be copying someone else's work (plagiarism) and you would fail your whole exam because of it. Model essays are useful to let you appreciate how and why such essays are marked, but your examination essays *must be your own work*.

The following is an example of an essay that would fulfil all the criteria of Intermediate 2. Do *not* try to learn it off by heart! However, look carefully at how it is structured, how it has an introduction and a conclusion and how quotations are worked into the paragraph structure.

Question

3 Choose a novel or short story which deals with a powerful human emotion, for example love, shame, hatred, fear, embarrassment, despair, joy, or any other strong emotion.

Show how the emotion you have chosen affects one, or more than one, of the characters and go on to show how it affects the course of the story.

Answer

Remote, by Bernard MacLaverty

Introduction: refers to the wording of the first two sentences of the question; gives the title (in inverted commas) and the author, plus a very brief summary of the plot

A story which deals with a powerful human emotion is 'Remote' by Bernard MacLaverty. Loneliness is the emotion portrayed in the character of an elderly widow, haunted by her husband's suicide.

Plot is related to the theme of loneliness. Expressions such as 'structured' and 'episode' relate to plot.

'Symbolism' is mentioned

The story is structured in such a way that the distressing details of the tragedy in the woman's life are gradually revealed. The first episode involves her getting a lift to the village from a visiting bird-watcher in his Land Rover so she can post a letter. When the man asks conversationally what her husband did, meaning his occupation, she replies without apparent emotion, 'He drowned himself in the loch.' Although the man clearly does not want to hear more, she adds that he did it 'on Christmas Day', saying that he was 'mad in the skull – away with the fairies'. The man becomes tongue-tied and apologetic: 'I'm sorry', and he drops her off quickly, leaving her to go up the 'steep hill' to the Post Office on foot. The 'steep hill' seems symbolic of her hard, lonely life.

A knowledge of 'significant details' of the story is shown here, plus some analysis of the plot and evaluation of its effect on the reader.

'Contrast' is mentioned, and its effect.

At the Post Office, she takes the letter outside before stamping it, and we guess this secretiveness may be because she is sending it to herself. This is sad as it implies she has no one to write to her. In the café, where she watches out for the postman from whom she will get her letter, Christmas carols are playing which trigger memories of her husband's death. It is clear that although her husband has been dead 'this long time', it is still fresh in her mind, and she remembers the awful way in which he made sure of dying by attaching 'two car batteries to his wrists'. The fact that her husband's suicide occurred on Christmas Day seems shocking as it is normally a happy festival when families get together. The Christmas decorations in the shops and cheery carols such as 'I Saw Mummy Kissing Santa Claus' contrast with the tragic associations she has with Christmas. This sets her apart from other people. When 'Silent Night' comes on the radio she leaves the café.

Characterisation is analysed. Quotation is used when analysing the force of certain expressions.

A sense of loneliness is conveyed through hints that her marriage was unhappy. She tells the bird-watcher she was 'lured' to the island 'forty-two years ago', revealing a sense of bitterness. In the café she recalls the 'black depression' which drove her husband to his death. The writer does not tell us if she contributed to her husband's depression at all or what happened on that fateful Christmas Day. She seems resentful of the 'dread' he subjected her to when he disappeared and the nuisance caused by his abandoned van: 'the thing had to be towed away'. We wonder what keeps her

Answer *continued* ➢

Answer continued

on the island which she seems to hate. The fact she is 'city born and bred' reveals how out of place she is, yet for some reason, perhaps guilt, she has never returned to the city. She admits to the bird-man that she misses her husband as a driver: 'There should always be one in the house who can drive'. This may symbolise her lack of direction without him.

Characterisation through relationships with other characters is explored.

The loneliness of her life is made clear in her relationships with other characters. Just as the bird-watcher quickly gets rid of her, the postman seems reluctant to take her home. He 'sighed' when she approaches him for a lift and seems ashamed to be seen with her: 'Wait for me round the corner.' He seems to delay as long as possible in picking her up. The writer emphasises her isolation by making the only named characters in the story people the woman hardly knows: Stuart the postman and Elizabeth at the Co-op check-out, who is unable to talk to her because of the queue of shoppers. The fact the woman herself is never named adds to the sense of alienation.

Setting, and symbolic significance of it.

'Personification' is mentioned.

A sense of physical isolation and loneliness is suggested by setting the story on an island. Certain details also seem symbolic. She goes down to the 'one-track' road which suggests the monotony of her life and the futility of her letter-writing with no one else to write back. The personification in the description of the peat-bog 'herring-boned with scars' suggests the pain of the traumatic events of her past life.

Language is now analysed in more detail.

Grammar and word choice.

The woman's loneliness is also emphasised through language. The singular in '*a* first-class stamp' and '*a* pork chop' pathetically reinforces how alone she is. In the café she has to 'treat herself' to a bun. Certain expressions reveal her dislike and distance from people. The bird-watcher is just called 'the bird-man' although she has had a lift from him several times, and she observes details of his appearance with disgust such as his 'unwashed hair', noting that he 'dressed like one of those hitch-hikers'.

Imagery: simile and its effect. This paragraph on the final part of the story acts as a suitable conclusion to the essay.

The last sentence sums up and refers back to the topic of 'powerful emotion'.

Most desolate of all are the final images in the story. She hears the geese on the loch sounding 'like a dance-hall full of people laughing and enjoying themselves, heard from a distance on the night wind'. This simile contrasts with her own loneliness and silence. The phrase 'from a distance' suggests her loneliness and remoteness from reality. The woman is waiting alone in the 'growing dark', an image which mirrors her life, which is likely to get more lonely as she grows more eccentric with age, caught up in her fantasy of the letters. MacLaverty thus rounds off his presentation of loneliness in a most powerful and disturbing way.

(900 words)

Chapter 7

WRITING A CRITICAL ESSAY ON DRAMA

This chapter will show you how to study a play and take you through the whole process from initial reading to writing a critical essay.

What is drama?

Here is one dictionary definition:

A piece of writing designed to be acted on stage. The story is told through dialogue and action. Costumes and scenery help to make the dramatisation more convincing.

There are numerous differences between telling a story in the form of a drama than in prose fiction (a novel or short story). Here are some of them:

- A novelist can spend more time on description of setting, atmosphere, characters.
- In drama most of the action is presented through dialogue between characters.
- To convey a character's inner thoughts, the technique of **soliloquy** is often employed. This is where the character is on stage alone, expressing his thoughts aloud.
- Plays are written to be performed rather than to be read as a text. Stage directions, lighting, an actor's tone of voice and gestures all have an important part to play. For this reason, it is always worth watching a film version of a play or, better still, a live performance on stage.

Many different plays are suitable for study at Intermediate 2 level, ranging from Shakespeare to present day texts.

Shakespeare's *Romeo and Juliet* has been used as an example in this chapter. However, as in all the chapters of this book which deal with literature, the techniques explained here can be applied to any suitable text.

Studying the play

On first reading

Initially you should simply try to establish *what happens* and *who's who*. Having read the play through (or, if you prefer, at the end of each act), write very brief notes on what has happened in each scene, without quotations.

You should also make a list of the characters and sum up in a few words what their role in the play is. If possible, do this in the form of a diagram, showing how the characters relate to each other.

Here is an example of how these two tasks could be done in relation to *Romeo and Juliet*.

Summary

Romeo and Juliet Act One

Scene 1: fight in street between servants of the two feuding families, the Montagues and Capulets. Fighting stopped by Prince Escalus. Introduction of Romeo, who is in love.

Scene 2: Capulet agrees to let Paris woo his fourteen year old daughter, Juliet. Capulet is organising a party; Romeo and Benvolio decide to gatecrash it, though they belong to the opposing family.

Scene 3: Lady Capulet tells Juliet about Paris' offer of marriage.

Scene 4: Mercutio's joking with Romeo and friends. Romeo has a premonition about the party that evening.

Scene 5: Romeo sees Juliet and they instantly fall in love. However, both then discover that they belong to opposing families and realise that the feud will spoil their chance of happiness.

***Who's who in* Romeo and Juliet**

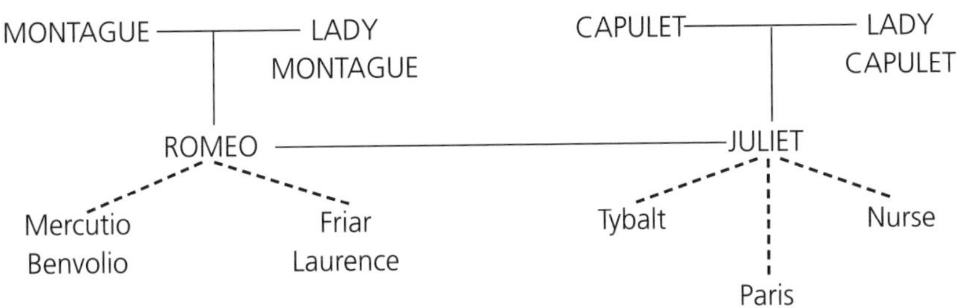

Compiling a scene-by-scene commentary

You should next aim to make more detailed notes on each scene of the play. Your teacher will guide you through the text in detail as part of your course of study. Alternatively, or in addition to this, you should make your own scene-by-scene notes.

Key Points

In each scene you should ask yourself questions such as:

- How important is this scene in the development of the plot? Is any new element introduced?
- What does this scene tell me about the main characters?
- Do any of the relationships develop?
- Does the scene shed light on any themes in the play?
- How would this scene come over on stage? Does it employ dramatic techniques such as suspense, conflict or soliloquy?

Hints and Tips

- Use sub-headings, numbers and bullet points. Solid pages of notes are hard to digest.
- Ensure that the main points are highlighted.
- Underneath the main points, include suitable back-up evidence including line references or quotations.
- Keep notes on plot to the minimum: focus on characters, themes, etc.

Example

The following page provides an example of how to lay out notes, based on the Prologue and opening scene of *Romeo and Juliet*.

Notes on *Romeo and Juliet*: Prologue and Act One, Scene One

Plot	Character	Theme	Other significant points
Prologue			
◆ Introduces setting: medieval Verona; two families in conflict. ◆ Reveals the ending of the play: lovers will take their own lives and feud will come to an end.		◆ Idea of fate is present right from the start of the play ('star-crossed lovers'). ◆ Themes of love and death introduced.	◆ Prologue suggests this is not a story where the reader is kept in suspense about the ending: knowing the tragic ending in advance affects our responses throughout.
Act One, Scene One			
◆ Fight in the street between servants of the Montagues and Capulets. ◆ Brought to a stop by Prince Escalus who issues an ultimatum: 'If ever you disturb our streets again/Your lives shall pay the forfeit of the peace'. ◆ Romeo is not involved, being more concerned with his personal problems.	**Tybalt** introduced: ◆ he enjoys violence for its own sake. **Romeo** introduced: ◆ He keeps apart from the fighting and 'shuts up his windows, locks fair daylight out'. ◆ He tells his friend Benvolio he is depressed as he is 'out of favour where I am in love'. ◆ Romeo comes over as being immature at this stage.	◆ Opening scene shows how the conflict between families affects the society of Verona at all levels: 'The quarrel is between our masters and us their men'. ◆ Structure of the scene (first half – feud; second half – Romeo in love) juxtaposes *[i.e. places side by side]* the contrasting ideas of hate and love, thus reinforcing the theme.	◆ A scene of violent action – typical of the atmosphere in Verona. ◆ Benvolio's advice to Romeo to forget about the girl he loves (Rosaline) and examine other beauties indirectly leads Romeo to go to Capulet's party where he meets his true love, Juliet.

For Practice

Write a similar scene-by-scene commentary on the rest of the play (or on the play you have been studying).

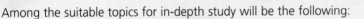

Detailed study of characters and themes

Once you have completed a detailed set of notes for the whole play you should have a sound understanding of what the text is all about and you will have plenty of material on which to base an essay.

However, simply learning up all this material is not enough. You are not likely to be asked to write a full act-by-act commentary on every aspect of the play (which is probably just as well!).

At this stage it is necessary to go through the whole play again, this time selecting only the scenes that are relevant to a particular topic. This may sound time-consuming, but there are likely to be several scenes that are not relevant to your chosen topic; in any case, to some extent you will simply be pulling together and 're-packaging' some of the observations you have already made in your scene-by-scene notes.

Key Points

Among the suitable topics for in-depth study will be the following:

- *Characters:* what are the main features of the personalities of the key figures in the play? How do these characters develop in the course of the play? What factors bring about these changes?
- *Relationships:* how do the main relationships develop? Is there conflict between characters' personalities and opinions? What factors cause the conflict and how is it resolved?
- *Themes:* is there an idea running through the whole play? (In *Romeo and Juliet* there is the love/hate theme, and the theme of fate; in other texts the theme might be something like revenge, prejudice, jealousy, ambition, exploitation or injustice).
- *Particular scenes:* is there a turning-point scene which has important consequences for the rest of the play? What is the importance of the opening and closing scene in the context of the whole action?

Example

One major topic in *Romeo and Juliet* is the development of the two main characters. Here is an example of how to make detailed notes on Romeo's development towards maturity.

Romeo's development towards maturity

- At first he seems rather **immature**, indulging in extreme melancholy from his unrequited passion for Rosaline. He upsets his family and his friends with his weeping and anti-social behaviour, deliberately seeking the dark as he 'shuts fair daylight out.'
- However, this behaviour is obviously out of character. His parents remark on it as being odd, and they cannot understand it. In the scene that takes place the morning after meeting Juliet, when he is joking with Mercutio and Benvolio, he is **cheerful and witty**, cleverly picking up on Mercutio's puns. From Mercutio's comment, 'Now art thou sociable! Now art thou Romeo!' we get the impression that this light-hearted behaviour shows the real Romeo.
- Romeo has a disturbing dream before going to Capulet's feast, and he has a **premonition** about what lies ahead, foreseeing his own fate and an 'untimely death', but he allows himself to be overruled by his friends.
- At the feast he shows he is changeable and **impulsive** as he immediately forgets Rosaline when he sees Juliet, and he instantly falls in love.
- Although he repeatedly comments on her beauty, he also shows respect for her, approaching her like a pilgrim to a saint: 'Make blessed my rude hand.' This shows more **dignity** and **depth of character** than we have seen until now.
- It is interesting to learn from his 'enemy', Old Capulet, that he has a good reputation: 'Verona brags of him / To be a virtuous and well-governed youth.' Since his enemy would tend to grudge him praise we believe this.
- In the famous balcony scene, Romeo again shows himself to be **passionate** and **impulsive**, leaping the orchard walls, risking being punished or even killed by the Capulets. When Juliet asks him how he got in, he replies light-heartedly and romantically: 'With love's light wings did I o'erperch these walls.' When she asked by whom he was directed there, he answers humorously: 'By Love.' He shows himself to be totally euphoric with love: 'O blessed, blessed night.' He is willing to take risks, but Juliet is more practical and anxious for his safety.
- When he comes to the Friar to ask him to perform the marriage, he tries to hurry him: 'I stand on sudden haste.' This **impatience** is attractive, but dangerous. He shows a rash tendency to tempt fate, saying at his wedding, 'Let love-devouring Death do what he will.'
- In the fatal brawl scene, Romeo is a **peace-maker** at first, refusing to rise to Tybalt's taunts. He bravely tries to intervene when Mercutio and Tybalt fight, sensibly warning them of the Prince's ruling. When Mercutio is killed, Romeo explains 'I thought all for the best.' Romeo **believes he is Fortune's victim**: 'This day's black fate', but he forgets he has also had good Fortune in marrying Juliet. He makes the fatal rash decision to avenge Mercutio out of pride: 'my reputation stained with Tybalt's slander.' He rushes into this without thinking of the consequences: 'fire-eyed fury be my conduct now.'

***Example** continued* ➢

Other questions on individual scenes include 'choose a play which has an important scene at a turning point in the play', 'choose a play which has a dramatic final scene' and 'choose a scene from a play in which a conflict between two characters reaches a climax'.

Questions on characters

These may be on an individual character or on the development of a relationship between characters.

Example

(a) on an individual character

Choose a play in which one of the main characters has to cope with strong feelings such as love, jealousy, ambition, hatred.

Show how the character deals with these feelings and what effect this has on the outcome of the play. (2005)

Example

(b) on relationships between characters

Choose a play in which one of the characters suffers a breakdown in a relationship with another character.

Show what the relationship was and go on to explain what makes it break down.

(2003 Specimen Question Paper)

You should refer directly to the words of the question at the start of the essay: in the case of the first example above, define the strong feelings.

Discuss in some detail how the chosen personality trait is seen in the character's words and actions. As in the scene questions, note that you should not only discuss the individual character, but show how his/her behaviour affects the events of the play and other characters. When writing about Romeo, for example, you should examine his relationship with Juliet, and with people who oppose him such as Tybalt.

Questions on themes

Example

Choose a play in which one of the main concerns is injustice or cruelty or exploitation or betrayal.

State the main concern and go on to show how the playwright deals with this concern in such a way as to involve your sympathies. (2003 Specimen Question Paper)

Other similar theme questions include: 'choose a play which deals with an important human issue: for example, war, crime, teenage rebellion, family conflict' and 'choose a play with a violent theme'.

This time, try to work out for yourself the guidance contained in the wording of the question.

Sample Critical Essay

Health Warning: Using model essays wrongly can be very bad for your exam results! You should never try to 'learn a model essay' for an English exam (either from this book or from any other source, such as the Internet), because you would be copying someone else's work (plagiarism) and you would fail your whole exam because of it. Model essays are useful to let you appreciate how and why such essays are marked, but your examination essays *must be your own work*.

The following is an example of an essay that would fulfil all the criteria of Intermediate 2. Do *not* try to learn it off by heart! However, look carefully at how it is structured, how it has an introduction and conclusion and how quotations are worked into the paragraph structure.

Question

Choose a play which has an important scene at a turning point in the play.

Give a brief account of the scene and go on to show why it is important in the play as a whole. (2003)

(You should also remember the general instruction that applies to all questions in the Drama section of the paper: answers to questions in this section should refer to the text and to such relevant features as: characterisation, key scene(s), structure, climax, theme, plot, conflict, setting . . .)

Answer

Romeo and Juliet Act Two, Scene Two – the Balcony Scene

An important scene which is a turning point in *Romeo and Juliet* by William Shakespeare is the balcony scene in Act Two.

Introduction: refers to the words of the question.

Romeo, after leaving the ball where he has met and fallen in love with Juliet, has given the slip to Mercutio, Benvolio and his other friends and he has climbed the high walls of the Capulets' orchard in the hope of seeing Juliet again. He discovers her on her balcony, where she is pondering aloud on their newly found love, and the dilemma of his being the son of her 'great enemy'.

Brief account, as required by the question.

The scene is important to the play as a whole as the pair agree to marry in secret the next day, which speedily advances the action towards the fateful events which will destroy them. This scene also reveals contrasts between the personalities of the two which is fascinating to the audience, and it is presented in language and imagery which illuminate the themes of the play.

Summary of points which the rest of the essay will examine in more depth.

Firstly, the scene marks an important stage in the development of the plot. Romeo belongs to the Montagues and Juliet to the Capulets, two families who maintain a centuries-old feud. This 'ancient grudge' has recently erupted again with a great street battle in which the Prince himself has intervened. The pair must therefore keep their meeting secret as they know their love will be forbidden, and Romeo's presence in Capulet territory brings tension to the play. Juliet tells him 'the place is death, considering who thou art.' The audience is intrigued by the twist of fate which has ironically caused the heirs of the families which hate one another to fall in love. We are also aware of the complication that Juliet's family is in the process of arranging a very advantageous marriage for her with a wealthy young nobleman, Count Paris. To try to outwit the opposition they know they will face, they agree to have 'the rite of marriage' performed next day. This hurry raises the tension as we are aware that they are playing with fire, a worry voiced by Juliet herself who admits it is 'too sudden'. Although the prologue has warned the audience that the pair will die, we find ourselves wishing them well as they impatiently put up with the 'sweet sorrow' of a few hours apart.

Topic sentence, making clear that this paragraph will discuss the importance of the scene to the development of the plot.

The scene is also important to the play as a whole in terms of characterisation. Shakespeare presents an interesting contrast between the personalities of the lovers. Juliet is practical and down to earth, while Romeo is a romantic and a reckless dreamer. She is surprised to see him as 'the orchard walls are high and hard to climb'. He jokes that he has flown over 'with love's light wings'. This makes him seem like Cupid, the god of love himself, which is a fanciful image. When she warns him

Topic sentence, referring back to the question and introducing the second main topic: how the scene is important in terms of characterisation.

Answers continued ➢

Answer continued

seriously that her kinsmen will 'murder' him, he boldly claims he is 'proof' against any danger as long as she loves him. When she asks who directed him to her window he teases her saying, 'Love'. It is Juliet who arranges the practical details: 'At what o'clock tomorrow shall I send to thee?' She also shows a sensible attitude to the speed of the action, describing it as 'too rash, too unadvised'. She seems much more mature than the submissive girl she was at the start of the play, and more realistic and serious than the impetuous, light-hearted Romeo.

Quotations used to back up points made.

The language which the lovers use in the scene is very touching. Their love is given dignity by their use of religious imagery which makes it seem like a valuable and sacred thing. Romeo seems to worship Juliet, calling her 'bright angel' and 'dear saint'. He calls the night 'blessed'. When she calls to him he says, 'It is my soul', as if they are so much in harmony they are like one and the same person. Imagery of light and the heavens is used effectively. When Romeo sees Juliet on her balcony he says,

Question allows 'any other appropriate feature' to be discussed. The essay writer has chosen to examine the style of language used in this scene.

> 'What light from yonder window breaks?
> It is the east and Juliet is the sun.'

This is a moving image, showing that he sees her as the centre of his world and a source of all goodness. Her eyes are compared to stars. She compares her love to the sea 'for both are infinite', an image suggesting power and strength. Another poignant image is her comparison of Romeo to a pet bird, but she fears she would love him too much and 'kill thee with much cherishing'. This hints at the tragic outcome of their love.

In the balcony scene, the dialogue of the lovers is interrupted at points by the voice of the Nurse, shouting 'Madam'. This is symbolic of the way in which the outside world will intrude upon their love and eventually destroy it. This serves to remind the audience of the ominous warning at the start of the play which tell us that the lovers are 'star-crossed', and they will be the victims of an unkind fate.

Thus, the balcony scene is a key scene in the play for several reasons: the lovers' decision to marry affects the development of the rest of the plot; the scene sheds light on the different personalities of Romeo and Juliet, while the poetic language helps us to understand the depth of their love.

Concluding paragraph sums up main points.

(887 words)

Chapter 8

WRITING A CRITICAL ESSAY ON FILM AND TV DRAMA

The Critical Essay paper in the Intermediate 2 exam also offers the choice of writing about a **film** or **TV drama**. A TV drama is defined as '**a single play, series or serial**'.

Common Mistakes

Warning: do **not** choose this option unless you are fully prepared for it!

In the past, media questions have often been attempted by poorly prepared, panicky students who find they cannot remember the literature texts they have read and instead write about a film or TV programme they may have watched the night before because the question seems 'easy'.

Only attempt a media question on a film or TV drama which you have studied in detail. Your teacher or tutor will be able to provide advice, and this book will also provide guidelines. If you *do* choose a critical essay from this section, it is important that you know and can apply the correct critical and technical terms for the discussion of such a text.

Hints and Tips

Question Choice

The questions on Film and TV Drama (formerly called Mass Media) in the first few years of Intermediate 2 were very limited in scope and number. Questions were on **either** a film **or** a TV drama. This meant that out of the three questions in the section, you might have a choice of only one on film. Such restriction of choice means you should be cautious about selecting this section of the paper, as more conventional choices such as poetry, prose and drama offer a wider range of questions. It is very important to choose a question that is appropriate to your text, and you are more likely to find one when there are more questions to choose from.

However, since 2004, most questions have begun with the words '**Choose a film or TV drama ...**' The range of questions has therefore become a little wider in recent years, and so a film could be a good option to choose, although, as in the case of literary texts, some films are more suitable than others for in-depth study.

Question Format

The format of the Film and TV Drama questions is the same as for those on written texts, which was discussed on pages 60–61.

- The section will be headed by a box containing recommended features to include in your discussion:

> Answers to questions in this section should refer to the text and to such relevant features as: use of camera, key sequence, characterisation, mise-en-scéne, editing, setting, music/sound effects, plot, dialogue . . .

- The **first** sentence will begin with an invitation to **choose** a film or TV drama, followed by a restriction on the choice such as, 'in which the portrayal of setting is very important'.
- The **second** sentence will give you the topic on which you must focus your essay.

Choosing a Suitable Text

If your teacher or tutor is preparing you for the Film and TV Drama option, he or she will select and recommend suitable examples to you. These will include works by respected directors, whose work not only deals with interesting themes but also uses intelligent scripts and employs skilful cinematography. In the case of television, work by writers such as Stephen Poliakoff and Dennis Potter, or adaptations of classic novels by Andrew Davies would offer the required features.

In the case of films, the work of directors such as Peter Weir (e.g. *Picnic at Hanging Rock*; *Dead Poets Society*) or Alfred Hitchcock (e.g. *The Birds*; *Rear Window*) yields much that is worthy of discussion. Classic black and white films such as Carol Reed's *The Third Man* and *The Fallen Idol* would certainly fulfil all the criteria. Films with an obvious literary background are also to be recommended. Examples include Shakespeare adaptations such as Roman Polanski's *Macbeth or* the versions of *Romeo and Juliet* directed by Franco Zeffirelli or Baz Luhrmann.

Oscar winners are not all suitable, but an excellent choice would be the film which won the Oscar for best film in 1981, *Chariots of Fire*, directed by Hugh Hudson. This is the film which will be used by way of illustration in this chapter.

Technical Terms

Some of the terms which appear in the box at the top of the Film and TV Drama section will already be familiar to you as they are also relevant to Drama and Prose questions. These include **plot**, **characterisation** and **setting**. Other general terms which might be useful include **contrast**, **juxtaposition**, **flashback** and **structure**. The following list explains some of the more specific terms you will need.

Key Words and *Definitions*

animation: photographing still objects or drawings in a series to make them appear alive on film.

camera use:

(i) angles: the camera may film the action from straight-on or from behind, at right angles or obliquely from either side. It may be set at a high angle (looking down on the action) or a low angle (looking up at it). A 'crane shot' looks down on the action from high above it. A 'point-of-view' shot gives the impression of looking through the eyes of one of the characters.

(ii) movements: in a **pan** (short for panorama) the camera moves round as if watching, like a person turning his head; **tilt** – moves up or down; **tracking** – moves forwards or backwards to follow the action, as if on 'tracks'.

close-up: the head of actor(s) appears to fill the screen; (see **shot**).

computer-generated images: images which appear to be real but are not, such as crowds created from a few actors, or dinosaurs developed by modifying film of live animals. These are used for special effects.

credits: list of actors and crew members given at the beginning and ending of a film.

cross-cutting: editing by using alternate pieces of film to show different actions.

dissolve: when two shots gradually merge.

editing: (also known as **montage**) cutting and placing sections of film one after another to create particular effects.

fade: where a shot ends by gradually disappearing.

'filmic techniques': any techniques to do with film making: use of camera, music, etc. including all in this list of key words.

frame: what is contained within one 'shot' of the camera, like a painter's canvas. **Freeze frame** is when action is paused momentarily (giving the effect of a picture); used for different effects, such as stressing the importance of a moment in the action.

graphics: the style and size of letters used in opening titles and credits.

hooks: exciting or intriguing events which engage the audience and keep them watching.

***Key Words* and *Definitions* continued ➢**

Key Words and *Definitions* continued

lighting: may be hard (imitating bright daylight) or soft (filtered to suggest evening or a dimly lit interior). Note the angle from which the light comes, from front, side or back. **Chiaroscuro** is a term from art, and indicates strongly contrasting light and shade, popular in a genre known as '**film noir**', so called from the use of black shadows to create atmosphere.

mise-en-scène: the staging of each individual scene, including action, lighting, setting, costume etc.

opening titles: the presentation of the title of the film and the names of the main actors at the start of the film. Includes graphics (words) and the background to the words, which may be film or artwork.

scene: a segment of action in one particular time or place.

score: the music which forms part of the sound-track. You should note the composer's name.

screenplay: the script of the film. This will include stage directions as well as dialogue.

sequence: a particular section of action which deals with one event, but which could comprise several scenes, including those which lead up to or follow the main piece of action.

shot: what is visible to the camera, defined by how large human figures appear on screen:

- **extreme long shot**: shows a landscape, with human figures appearing complete and small.
- **long shot**: shows whole human figure
- **medium shot**: shows approximately half the human figure
- **medium close-up**: head and shoulders
- **close-up**: head fills screen
- **extreme close-up**: detail such as eyes or mouth fills screen; details and textures become important.

slow motion: action shown slower than actual speed to achieve special effects.

soundtrack: all the sound of a film, including dialogue, music and sound effects.

special effects: spectacular representations of explosions, supernatural happenings, battles, space travel etc. Often computer generated.

still: a single frame from a film used as a photograph for publicity.

take: one single piece of filming, made without stopping the camera or the action.

voice-over: a character or narrator speaks without being seen, sometimes providing a commentary on or explanation of the action.

Studying a film or TV drama

The following stage-by-stage plan can be applied to any suitable text. The film *Chariots of Fire* has been used as an example in the 'suggested responses' section and for the specimen essay but any suitable text could be approached in the same way.

Study programme for Film or TV Drama

First Viewing

Watch the whole film once. At this stage, concentrate on the film as a complete text, and take only brief notes as you view. Then,

a) make some initial notes on:
   - themes
   - characters
   - the main settings

b) write an outline of the story

c) note down particularly memorable events or sequences which you can look at in detail later.

Second Viewing

Watch the film again. Pause it from time to time to make notes on how the film is structured, and note any particularly striking use of the technical devices from the list on pages 107–108.

Third Viewing

Select one or two sequences for particular attention. A good range would include the opening sequence, one or two central ones, and the closing sequence. Look at those in detail, using the pause button frequently, and write a description of filmic techniques you notice. Note down any useful quotations from the script.

Suggested responses to this study programme on the film *Chariots of Fire* are given on pages 111–113.

Attempting a Question

Choose a question from a past paper and write a practice answer. Here are four examples of questions to choose from, with tips on how to approach them.

(You should also remember the general instructions that apply to all questions in the Film and TV Drama section of the paper: answers to questions in this section should refer to the text and to such relevant features as: use of camera, key sequence, characterisation, mise-en-scéne, editing, setting, music/sound effects, plot, dialogue . . .)

Questions

1 Choose an opening sequence from a film which is immediately effective in holding your attention and establishing information vital to your understanding of the film.

By analysing this sequence show how it is effective in establishing important elements of the film.

***Questions** continued* ➢

Questions continued

2 Choose a film which has an important sequence involving thrilling action such as a chase, a fight, an ambush or a supernatural event.

Briefly say why the sequence is important, and show how the sequence is made exciting to the audience.

3 Choose a film in which the closing sequence makes use of a variety of film techniques to make its dramatic impact.

Briefly state what happens in the closing sequence and show how the techniques used make the ending dramatic.

4 Choose a film in which there is a sequence of great importance to the development of character and/or plot.

Show how elements of character and/or plot are developed in this sequence to create impact.

Question 1 'An effective opening sequence'

This is quite a complex question as it sets two tasks: you must consider why the opening is both gripping and informative. You must therefore show how the filmic techniques provide effective 'hooks' to engage the interest of the audience, and also how the opening sequence provides clues to what happens in the film so that the audience will understand the story, both in terms of plot and themes.

Question 2 'A thrilling action sequence'

This is a fairly straightforward question; any exciting sequence would do. The 'importance' refers to the context of the sequence within the complete film: you must explain how it fits into the story as a whole and contributes to the development of the plot or characters. You should concentrate on filmic techniques in explaining how the director has made the sequence 'thrilling'.

Question 3 'Dramatic techniques in a closing sequence'

Again this is quite a straightforward question: you must show why the ending of the film is effective dramatically. You should concentrate on filmic techniques to show why the close of the film has 'impact'. Remember that this question could also refer to an emotional impact on the audience, not simply an ending which is an exciting climax.

Question 4 'Development of character and/or plot in a sequence'

Remember to place your sequence in context i.e. show where it comes in the film. You are given a choice of looking only at characters, or only at plot or at a combination of the two. This is a very suitable question for *Chariots of Fire*: an excellent choice of sequence would be the one where Eric Liddell is called in front of the British Olympic committee at the Embassy ball.

You can compare your essay with the specimen essay on pages 114–115.

Suggested Responses to Study Programme on *Chariots of Fire*

First viewing

Themes
Winning and losing; living by one's principles; coping with prejudice; the impact of religion on people's lives; amateur/professional attitudes.

Characters

- Harold Abrahams: from wealthy Jewish family, educated at Cambridge. Very intense and determined to prove himself; sensitive to anti-Semitism; volatile and moody, but he enjoys singing and light opera. Prepared to adopt professional help to win.
- Eric Liddell: calm, high-principled Scotsman, born in China to missionary family. Running is an extension of his religion, as he can 'feel God's pleasure'. Refuses to run on a Sunday, even when pressured by very important people.
- Aubrey Montague: friend of Harold at Cambridge; loses his race, but is respected as a well-balanced friend by Abrahams. Provides commentary in places through his letters home delivered in voice-over.
- Lord Andrew Lindsay: cheerful, aristocratic, friend of Harold and Aubrey at Cambridge; runs 'for fun'; wins silver medal in Games, showing he takes running less seriously than Harold or Eric.
- Sybil Gordon: actress; girlfriend of Harold Abrahams.
- Jennie Liddell: Eric's very religious sister who initially opposes his running.
- Sam Mussabini: Harold Abrahams' coach.

Settings
Scotland; Cambridge; Paris for the 1924 Olympic Games.

Outline of the story
Eric Liddell and Harold Abrahams both come separately to prominence as runners. Eric meets some opposition from his sister who would like him to devote all his time to their Christian

mission, but convinces her when he says he wishes to do the running first, since God has made him fast 'for a purpose'. Harold Abrahams attends Caius College, Cambridge, where he encounters a degree of anti-Semitism which motivates him to win on the athletics field. He falls in love with an actress, Sybil Gordon, whom he gets to know at the theatre.

The first time Liddell and Abrahams meet in a race, Liddell wins. Sam Mussabini, an athletics coach, offers to train Abrahams. This is disapproved of at Cambridge, as being inconsistent with the amateur ideal. Both Liddell and Abrahams are selected for the British Olympic team in 1924, along with three of Abrahams' Cambridge colleagues – Lord Lindsay, Aubrey Montague and Henry Stallard.

In Paris, a dilemma arises when Liddell discovers the heat of his race, the 100 metres, is to be held on a Sunday. He refuses to run, even though pressure is brought to bear by the British Olympic committee, along with the Prince of Wales. However, Lord Lindsay, who has already won a silver medal, offers to yield his place in the 400 metres to Liddell. Although he has not trained for this distance, Liddell wins to great acclaim. After losing to the Americans in the 200 metres, Abrahams wins the 100 metres.

Memorable sequences

- Opening sequence at memorial service for Harold Abrahams.
- Sequence in the training camp in Kent, including the cricket match in the hotel ballroom.
- The 'College Dash' where Abrahams and Andrew Lindsay attempt to race round the quad at Caius College while the clock is striking twelve.
- The Highland Gathering, where Liddell is presenting prizes and wins a quarter mile race. The sequence ends next morning with him reprimanding little boys for playing football on a Sunday.
- Liddell's race at Murrayfield in the international between Scotland and France where he falls, but gets up to win the race.
- The Athletics Championship race in London where Liddell and Abrahams race against each other for the first time, won by Liddell.
- Scene where the Cambridge masters invite Abrahams to dinner to reprimand him for his 'professional attitude'. Abrahams storms out but is immediately met by his friends who tell him they have all been selected for Paris.
- The confrontation between Liddell and the Olympic committee, ending with Lindsay's solution to the dilemma.
- Abrahams' 100 metre race and his reaction after winning.
- Liddell's 400 metre race.

Second viewing

Structure

The film begins at the memorial service in 1978 for Harold Abrahams who will be one of the main characters in the film. Flashback is used as the film cuts to young men training by the sea back in 1924. At the end there is a flash forward to the memorial service again, giving a circular structure, with the church service acting as a frame for the main action. The final credits return to the film of the characters as young men training on the beach against Vangelis' rousing 'Chariots of Fire' theme music, repeating the opening sequence.

The internal structure of the film is complex. Cross-cutting between the stories of Liddell in Scotland and Abrahams in England leads up to their first athletic confrontation in London.

The film is also structured through a series of races. Interesting contrasts are created; e.g. the 'College Dash' around a Cambridge quadrangle with athletes in perfect white kit, ending with champagne, juxtaposed to the next race of little boys in tweed shorts in the highlands of Scotland.

The first half of the film follows the careers of the two main athletes and their training; the second half focuses on the events of the Paris Olympics – on Liddell's crisis of conscience and Abrahams' ambition to beat the Americans.

Technical devices
Presentation of the races using a variety of techniques – editing film from different camera angles; slow motion; use of close-ups; repeating the action.

Some clever editing – Master's comment on Abrahams' success as the first man in 700 years to achieve the 'college dash': 'I doubt there's a faster man in the kingdom' cuts to Liddell in a remote part of Scotland a year later. This is ironic as Liddell will go on to beat Abrahams.

A photographer taking a photograph of the Cambridge relay team dissolves to the actual photograph in a newspaper; the arrival of the Americans in Paris to a band playing cuts to the same film as a black and white silent newsreel being shown in a Paris cinema and being watched and commented on by the British athletes.

Sample Critical Essay

Health Warning: Using model essays wrongly can be very bad for your exam results! You should never try to 'learn a model essay' for an English exam (either from this book or from any other source, such as the Internet), because you would be copying someone else's work (plagiarism) and you would fail your whole exam because of it. Model essays are useful to let you appreciate how and why such essays are marked, but your examination essays *must be your own work*.

The following is an example of an essay that would fulfil all the criteria of Intermediate 2. Do *not* try to learn it off by heart! However, look carefully at how it is structured, how it has an introduction and conclusion and how quotations are worked into the paragraph structure.

Question

Choose a film which has a powerful scene in which a strong human emotion such as love or hate or terror is portrayed.

Show how the emotion of the scene is important to the theme of the film, and how the emotion is emphasised for you by the filmic techniques used.

Answer

A film which contains a scene portraying a strong human emotion is *Chariots of Fire*, directed by Hugh Hudson; a 'biopic' which won the 'best film' Oscar in 1981. The film depicts the careers of two athletes, Harold Abrahams, played by Ben Cross, and Eric Liddell, played by Ian Charleson, who compete in the 1924 Olympic Games. A highly emotional scene occurs when the two runners compete against each other for the first time, and Abrahams is plunged into despair when he loses. The desire to win is one of the main themes of the film.

Introduction gives title and director, and basic information about chosen film; one particular scene is selected; powerful emotion is identified as despair at losing; theme introduced as the desire to win.

Prior to this scene, the film has shown the two runners developing individually to international level, Liddell in Scotland and Abrahams in Cambridge. Sequences showing their personal triumphs are crosscut to emphasise the great difference in their routes to success. These sequences also reveal their contrasting motivation as runners. Liddell is a committed Christian, who 'feels God's pleasure' when he runs. Abrahams is the son of 'a Lithuanian Jew', an immigrant who has made a fortune as a financier. Abrahams is very sensitive to anti-Semitism and he runs as a means of both confronting and coming to terms with prejudice.

Chosen scene is placed in context of whole film; comments on characterisation are expanded to show development of theme.

The scene in which the two men meet in a race for the first time is highly emotional, as one is destined to lose. In the opening mise-en-scène, hard lighting is used for the open-air setting with a straight on camera angle to show six runners, in long shot, lining up at the start of the race. All are wearing white vests and shorts, except Liddell, the second from right, who is wearing a dark blue Scottish vest. This visual clue singles him out as being different, and suggests that he will win.

Analysis of chosen scene begins with topic sentence.

Filmic techniques mentioned: lighting; mise-en-scene; use of camera and visual hooks.

Off-camera, the starter's voice is heard and after a brief moment of suspense as the runners 'take their marks', the shot of the starting gun marks the beginning of the 100 yard race. It takes place in real time, lasting approximately 10 seconds and is filmed in one take. The camera tracks back and up to a crane shot so that we look down on the runners as they cross the finishing line, an angle which shows Liddell clearly in front. The film then cuts to a half length shot of Lord Lindsay, a fellow athlete and Cambridge friend of Abrahams, who says 'Extraordinary', reflecting shock that the star English athlete, reckoned to be 'the fastest man in the kingdom', has been beaten.

Techniques used to present the race, the loss of which will arouse the emotion of despair. Camera angles make it very clear who has won.

The director now begins to concentrate directly on showing Abrahams' disappointment. The finish of the race is shown again, but in slow motion, ending with a three quarter shot of Abrahams showing his desperate attempt to catch Liddell at the finishing-tape. Then the camera zooms in to a close-up of his highly expressive, distraught face.

Filmic techniques used to express an emotion.

Answer *continued* ➢

Answer continued

The final part of the scene now moves forward an hour or so in time. The grandstand of the stadium is shown in long shot with a single figure dressed in a suit sitting motionless towards the back of the stand which is in shadow. The camera zooms in slightly to show the figure is Abrahams. An effective sound effect is used, a slow, rhythmic banging, like nails being driven into a coffin lid, reflecting Abrahams' belief that his athletic career is over. The camera pans round to show the sound is being created by a steward flipping up the wooden seats. Music is introduced to match the mood – descending scales played on strings have a melancholy effect. Close-ups of Abrahams' unhappy face are repeatedly cross-cut with slow motion scenes of the end of the race showing his anguished expression and Liddell's winning shout. In this way the director emphasises how Abrahams is brooding over the fact that he lost the race.

Use of sound, music and camera techniques described in this paragraph.

The camera then pans round from a close-up of Abrahams to show that Abrahams' girl-friend, Sybil Gordon, has joined him. She tries to cheer him up by saying, 'It's a race you've lost, not a relation. Nobody's dead.' Abrahams remains inconsolable: 'I lost'. The theme of winning and losing is central to the film. Eric Liddell is prepared to give up the chance of winning when it appears he must run a race on a Sunday – to him, his religious principles are more important than winning. Lord Lindsay explained that he runs 'for fun'. To Abrahams, winning is everything: 'If I can't win, I won't run'.

Theme of desire to win developed in analysis of Abraham's response to losing. Quotations from dialogue develop the theme.

The scene ends on a lighter note as the small comic figure of the coach Sam Mussabini appears in long shot between Sybil and Harold, saying 'I can find you another two yards.' A further touch of comedy is introduced as he touches his hat roguishly. Mussabini had previously turned down the offer to coach Abrahams, but he has changed his mind on viewing this encounter. This provides a link to the next sequence of the film which shows their training programme. This relationship between Abrahams and Mussabini is relevant to the theme of winning and losing as Abrahams shows he is willing to do anything to win. He lays himself open to accusations of professionalism, which the Masters at Cambridge consider contrary to the Olympic spirit and the amateur ideal.

Scene linked to rest of film.

The impact of the sequence depicting the race between Liddell and Abrahams lies in the director's use of filmic techniques to show the powerful emotions of Abrahams. The audience cannot fail to be moved, whether they agree with his fanatical desire to win or not.

Concluding reference to topics of question: strong emotion and theme.

(911 words)

Chapter 9

WRITING A CRITICAL ESSAY ON LANGUAGE

The language option in the Critical Essay paper was introduced in 2003 and is thus a relatively recent addition to Intermediate 2.

Should I choose a question from the new 'Language' section?

If you are fully prepared for a language question then there is no reason why you should not choose it. Do **not** choose a question which you feel you could answer without preparation – this will be an illusion. You should be aware that the Language option is chosen by only a small minority of candidates.

You should be aware of the unpredictable nature of the questions in the Language option and you may wish to consider selecting the more conventional options of Poetry, Prose and Drama or even the Film and TV Drama option, if you have prepared a suitable text.

What do the language questions deal with?

What You Should Know

The topics covered by the questions in the Language section of the Critical Essay paper include:

- the language spoken in a particular area (dialect)
- the language spoken by a particular age group (register)
- the language spoken by a particular group of people, such as those with a common leisure interest (register)
- the language of persuasion – advertisements (both public and private)
- the language of TV and radio
- the language of the Internet
- the language of newspapers and magazines

Question Format

The format of the questions in the Language option is similar to those in the Literature sections.

As in the case of the other sections, there will be a box at the start recommending features to include in your essay:

> Answers to questions in this section should refer to the text and to such relevant features as: register, accent, dialect, slang, jargon, vocabulary, tone, abbreviation . . .

Again, there will be three questions to choose from. Each question will contain two sentences.

The first sentence will begin with the word, '**Choose ...**' and will go on to mention an aspect of written or spoken language.

The second sentence will define your task. For example, in the 2005 paper, one task was to compare the effectiveness of the language of two advertisements of your choice.

Key Words and Definitions

Terms Specific to Language Questions

abbreviations: shortened versions of words, typical of informal language

accent: pronunciation of words

caption: a phrase heading an advertisement or attached to a photograph or illustration

dialect: style of language used in a geographically defined area, including accent, vocabulary and grammar

emotive language: language which aims to arouse emotions such as anger or compassion

graphics: drawings or photographs which accompany a piece of writing

headlines: words at the top of a newspaper article in bold type

imagery: similes and metaphors

jargon: technical language used by a limited group of people

register: style of language used by a particular group of people

slogans: a distinctive phrase used for selling a product or advertising a company

sub-heading: a small headline within an article

Key Words and Definitions continued ➢

Key Words and Definitions continued

target audience: readership at which a piece of writing is aimed

tone: the expression of the writer's feelings or attitude to his subject

typography: style of print

white space: part of a page in a magazine or newspaper which does not contain text or graphics.

Choosing a Topic for Study

As mentioned earlier, the range of possible question topics is wide, and this makes it difficult to predict what may be asked in any given year.

One of the topics which has appeared regularly in the Language section of Paper 2 is the **language of persuasion** which is used in different types of advertisements.

Looking at the language of persuasion

From a range of good quality magazines, select 2–3 full page advertisements selling a product. Choose examples which include at least 150 words of text. Many advertisements aim to make the desired impact largely by photographs and graphics, but these would be unsuitable since your task requires you to analyse language. Note carefully which magazine(s) your chosen advertisements appear in.

Study the advertisements carefully, and then, for each example, write notes on the following:

1 The target audience

What kind of people would be likely to read the magazine the advertisement appeared in? What interests/jobs are they likely to have? How well off are they likely to be?

Hints and Tips

Examples of readers with special interests might be car enthusiasts (e.g. *What Car*) or keen travellers (e.g. *National Geographic*). Readers of the magazines which accompany the Sunday broadsheet newspapers (e.g. *The Sunday Times, The Observer, The Sunday Telegraph*) are likely to be well-educated and in higher income groups. Fashion magazines (e.g. *Vogue, Marie Claire*) are targeted at women who are very interested in clothes and make-up.

When considering the effect and likely appeal of the language of the advertisement, it is important to think of the people the advertiser is aiming at.

2 Captions and headlines

Most full page advertisements will include a photograph or graphics of some kind. These will be accompanied by a caption or headline in bold type. Captions may include **puns** (words/expressions with more than one meaning) or they may include language techniques such as **alliteration, rhetorical questions** or **emotive language**. The caption is likely to refer to the graphics, either directly or obliquely.

Consider how the photograph and the language of the caption provide a '**hook**' to attract the reader's attention.

3 Subheadings

The text is likely to be broken up into sections so that the reader can assimilate it easily.

Look at any subheadings (words in bold type, slightly smaller than the main caption) within the body of the text. How do they provide further 'hooks' to keep the reader interested? Consider the **sentence structures** they use. Do they include **questions/commands/exclamations**?

4 The main text

Try to identify and assess the effect of some of the following language techniques which are typical of this type of writing:

> **Sentence structures:** Look for constructions such as **commands**, **questions, exclamations** and **minor sentences** (sentences without verbs). Such constructions are typical of spoken English, and give writing the impact that makes it persuasive.

Positive word choice: words and expressions with **positive connotations** (pleasant associations) e.g. 'unique', 'special', 'supreme', 'beautiful', 'once-in-a-lifetime'. These expressions make the product, or the lifestyle associated with the product, seem desirable and so induce the reader to buy it. Look out for adjectives in **comparative** (ending **–er**) or **superlative** (ending **–est**) forms: e.g. nicer, quicker, longest, furthest.

Colloquial language: many advertisers use **abbreviations** and **slang** which will not only be easy for the reader to follow but will create a friendly tone.

Jargon: **technical** or **scientific language** appeals to like-minded people and will impress less knowledgeable people.

Tone:

- a **colloquial** tone is friendly and chatty and gives the impression of treating the reader like a friend. The pronoun 'you' is likely to be used, as the advertiser speaks directly to the reader.
- an **emotive** tone appeals to the feelings of the reader. Such feelings might be fear (e.g. promotion for an insurance company), guilt (e.g. appealing for money for a charity) or insecurity (e.g. cosmetics to conceal skin imperfections).
- a **scientific/technical** tone may try to impress the reader. Cosmetic adverts often take this tone, implying that great research has gone into a product. The use of jargon which the reader will not be familiar with is a common 'trick' in creating this tone.
- a **humorous** tone: a jokey style will put the reader in a good humour and coax them into buying the product.

5 The Company logo and slogan

All companies have a distinctive badge or 'logo'. Usually, it consists of a simple design. Consider how this might appeal to readers. A slogan may accompany the logo and give customers confidence in what they are buying.

In the advertisement on page 121, Royal Mail is advertising a presentation set of special issue stamps. Study the advertisement carefully by looking at the pictures and reading the text. Then answer the questions.

breathtaking

whichever way you look at it

There are some places on earth – both natural and man-made – that simply take your breath away. And now in a unique collaboration between Royal Mail and Australia Post, eight of these UNESCO World Heritage sites are being commemorated in a set of beautiful stamps.

Preserve the world's wonders

You can enjoy this special issue in a Presentation Pack, containing a set of the Royal Mail stamps together with fascinating information. And for the first time ever, there's a joint Presentation Pack, containing both the Royal Mail and Australia Post stamps.

Order today

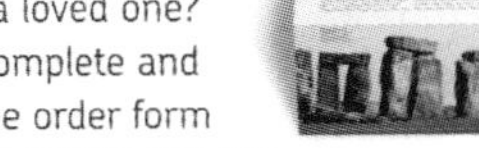

This memorable issue is set to be very popular, so why not order today, for yourself, or even a loved one? Simply complete and return the order form below, call **08457 641 641** or visit **www.royalmail.com/stamps**

with us it's personal™

Questions

1 The target audience

This advertisement appeared in the *National Geographic Magazine*, an expensive glossy magazine containing articles of geographical interest, illustrated with many eye-catching photographs.

- What kind of people would read such a magazine? What features of this advertisement would be likely to attract their attention?

2 The main photograph and the caption

- Explain what the photograph shows and why it would appeal to the target audience.
- Explain the meaning and effect of the caption (the words in bold type in the top half of the advertisement).
- What do the other graphics add to the impact of the advertisement?

3 The first paragraph

- Why will the first sentence appeal to the target audience?
- Find examples of words and expressions with positive connotations and briefly explain the effect of this.
- Find examples of words/ideas that will particularly appeal to the target audience, explaining why.
- How is the actual product introduced?

4 The second paragraph

- Look at the sub-heading 'Preserve the world's wonders'. Is there anything misleading about it?
- Select further examples of words with positive connotations.
- Is there any attempt at selling the product in this paragraph?

5 The third paragraph

- Compare the tone and style of this subheading with the previous one.
- What type of language is being used in the rest of this paragraph to urge the reader to buy the product?
- Pick out phrases and ideas which will appeal to the emotions of the readers.

6 The company logo and slogan

- In what way might the 'Royal Mail' logo with the crown and its slogan '*with us it's personal*' appeal to readers?

You can check your answers with the suggested responses on pages 123–124.

For Practice

Write an answer to this question which is slightly adapted from one which appeared in the 2005 Intermediate 2 Language option:

Choose **two** examples of language of advertisements.

By looking closely at the language of two advertisements, state which one you think is more effective in persuading you to buy the product.

Remember

Since this is a 'Language' option, you should not discuss the technical aspects of photographs and graphics, but look at them in conjunction with the accompanying text. The text often refers directly to the art work, so you should not ignore it.

Answers

Suggested Responses to Questions on pages 122.

1 The target audience

- The likely readership is well-educated people who are in higher economic groups, interested in exotic places and appreciative of the beauty of the natural world. Photographs of beautiful scenery and an invitation to admire it are likely to be effective 'hooks' to draw them in.

2 The main photograph and the caption

- The main photograph is a composite of two photographs, one of which is reversed. A photograph of Stonehenge is placed on top of a reversed photograph of Ayers Rock so that the sky looks like water and the rock appears to be a reflection. The typical National Geographic reader would be likely to recognise both the scenes and be intrigued by the trick photography. This 'hook' would lead the readers towards the product being sold.
- Both sights are 'breathtaking' individually, but the strange juxtaposition of the two is especially amazing, and so the top bold headline is appropriate. The caption 'whichever way you look at it' is a pun. It could mean 'whatever attitude you take to the world' or 'which way up you look at the picture'. The humour of this is likely to appeal to the reader and encourage them to read on.
- The sights pictured on the row of stamps are likely to interest the readers of this magazine. The small size will force them to look closely, as does the small facsimile of the information leaflet.

Answers *continued* ➢

Answers continued

3 The first paragraph

- The readers, as geography enthusiasts, are likely themselves to be travellers – or armchair travellers – and will empathise with this comment.
- 'take your breath away'; 'unique'; 'commemorated'; 'beautiful'. Such words subconsciously influence the reader with the suggestion of something special which they are now being offered the chance to own.
- Australia Post – refers to a foreign country with much spectacular beauty; UNESCO World Heritage Sites – conservation of beautiful places is likely to find sympathy with target audience; 'world heritage' suggests beauty on a global scale, which is impressive.
- The product is introduced subtly with the word 'collaboration' which lends a scholarly and even scientific tone and leads up to the 'set of beautiful stamps' which is the product, placed in a prominent stress position at the end of the paragraph.

4 The second paragraph

- 'Preserve the world's wonders' is likely to appeal to a lover of natural beauty. The concept is grand and honourable. However, it could be seen as misleading, as what is being offered is a set of stamps picturing these 'wonders'. At no point does it say Royal Mail or the purchasers of the stamps will contribute to conservation.
- 'enjoy'; 'special'; 'fascinating'; 'for the first time ever'.
- The product is being sold with the words 'you can enjoy', leading the reader to anticipate his feelings on purchasing it. The word 'you' speaks directly to the reader and contrasts with the more indefinite 'you' of the caption below the photograph.

5 The third paragraph

- 'Order today' is a command, consisting of an imperative verb + an adverb. The tone is blunt, forceful, demanding and unsubtle.
- More positive, tantalising expressions are used: 'this memorable issue'. There is a hint that the product is so desirable it will become scarce, suggesting the reader should buy at once while there is still time. The phrase 'why not order …' is more coaxing and polite in tone than the sub-heading. The language aims to make buying seem effortless: 'Simply complete and return …'
- 'set to be very popular' implies the reader will do something which others do, making them part of a group and suggesting buying is the right thing to do; 'for yourself' has a coaxing tone, appealing to idea of self-indulgence; 'a loved one' stirs the emotions of the reader, and suggests how they might please someone close to them.

6 The company logo and slogan

- The crown on the logo gives a suggestion of 'by royal appointment', although Royal Mail is now a private company. It lends respectability and a touch of class. The slogan 'with us it's personal' reassures customers they will be treated as individuals, and therefore valued. This helps to promise they will get good service.

Chapter 10

TECHNICAL ACCURACY

Punctuation

Running sentences together without full stops is perhaps the most common – and certainly the most serious – punctuation error. Remember: a completed statement that makes sense standing on its own should end with a full stop.

One place where people often put a comma where there should be a full stop is before the word '*this*':

Shakespeare reveals a contrast between the personalities of the lovers, this is interesting to the audience as it illustrates certain themes of the play.

You can avoid this fault by putting a full stop after 'lovers':

Shakespeare reveals a contrast between the personalities of the lovers. This is interesting to the audience as it illustrates certain themes of the play.

Alternatively, change 'this' to 'which':

Shakespeare reveals a contrast between the personalities of the lovers which is interesting to the audience as it illustrates certain themes of the play.

Take care with apostrophes

Some people think that an apostrophe should be stuck onto any word that ends with an 's'!

Apostrophes are used to indicate possession or ownership. The apostrophe comes *before* the 's' if the word is singular and *after* the 's' if the word is plural.

The word which causes the most confusion is *its*. Only put in an apostrophe when *it's* is short for 'it is'. When ownership is involved, *its* does not have an apostrophe.

Spelling

- You should make a list of the words that you have always found hard to spell. Copy out these words several times, concentrating on the particular letters that cause you difficulty.
- Many spelling errors are a result of carelessness. Watch out for words that are easily mixed up, such as *there/their*, *to/too/two*, *were/where*.
- There are some words that you are almost certainly going to use in a literature essay. Make sure you can spell the names of all the figures of speech, for instance.

'Onomatopoeia' is the most difficult one! Remember there are four 'o's in this word. 'Simile' has no 'i' between the 'l' and the 'e'. You are also likely to use words such as *effective*, *character*, *development*, *emphasis* (noun), *emphasise* (verb), *technique*, and so on.

Paragraphing

It is easy to let your thoughts run on and to forget to divide the essay into paragraphs. Lack of paragraphing suggests that the essay does not develop in a logical, stage-by-stage fashion, but the writer just pours everything out at once.

Remember to begin a paragraph with a **topic sentence** which gives a general overview of what the paragraph deals with. Don't begin with a specific, detailed point.

Expression

In Close Reading papers, examiners give 1 mark for one point and then add up the total. In an essay, though, an overall mark is arrived at by assessing such things as knowledge of the text, use of evidence and fluency of expression. Consider the following aspects of your written style.

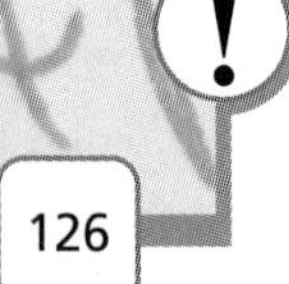

Avoid being repetitive

- Have you used the same word or words several times in one paragraph? Try to think of synonyms (words with the same meaning). Note how in the sample essay on the poem the opening sentence refers to:

a poem which starts off by describing an everyday incident

while the second paragraph says:

The poem begins by depicting a common event

The meaning is the same, but the expression is different.

- If you find yourself saying something like 'as I mentioned earlier', then stop and think: are you just repeating yourself unnecessarily? The problem may be that you have not grouped your ideas on one topic together. Deal with everything you want to say about one aspect in one place and then move on to the next aspect.

Link your points

- Essays often read like a disjointed series of separate points. Avoid this by creating links using expressions such as:

  for example
  another technique used is …
  moreover
  in addition to
  however
  in contrast
  most importantly
  thus
  therefore

- You should, however, avoid the stereotyped *firstly*, *secondly*, *thirdly*, *finally* approach. Numbering points is very useful for note-making but is not recommended in an essay.

Stick to a formal style

In the section on Close Reading we considered the differences between formal and informal language (page 15). An essay should be written in a **formal** way.

- Avoid abbreviations. Write out words like *don't* and *isn't* in full.
- Avoid the informal second person 'you'. Rather than saying 'the writer tells you that …' say 'the writer tells the reader that …'
- Avoid slang or conversational expressions.
- Exclamation marks also give an informal, light-hearted tone and should generally be avoided in a critical essay.

GLOSSARY

This glossary lists explanations of terms and expressions which may appear in the exam questions, as well as definitions of technical terms which you may wish to use in your own Close Reading answers and Critical Essays.

alliteration: repetition of initial and sometimes internal consonant sounds in a phrase.

anecdote: a small story, often personal, included to illustrate an idea in a larger piece of work.

anticlimax: a sudden falling off at the end of a list which builds up in rank or significance; a sudden relaxation of tension.

characterisation: the creation and presentation of characters (people) in a text.

climax: the culminating point in a list of things which builds in rank or significance; the peak of tension.

context: the immediate surroundings of a word or phrase; or the precise place in which it is used.

emotive: extreme language which stirs emotion in the reader, such as anger or compassion.

expression: '*an* expression' means a word or, more usually, a phrase; otherwise 'expression' means style of writing.

features of style: a vague and all-inclusive expression, which can cover word choice, sentence structure, imagery, tone, figures of speech, humour, use of examples, etc. (see *techniques*).

figurative language: alternative word for *metaphor*; contrasts with literal (actual) meaning.

figure of speech: general term for language techniques such as simile, metaphor, hyperbole, alliteration, oxymoron, irony, etc.

first person: using 'I', 'we' instead of 'he', 'they' etc. The writer appears to be talking to the reader.

flashback: a technique of structure where events move back to an earlier time.

hyperbole: exaggeration for dramatic or humorous effect.

illustration: not a picture, but a detailed example or a small story which acts as an example.

image: an unlike thing which something is compared to – it will have one or more points of similarity. In the expression 'the soldier was as brave as a lion', the image is 'lion', a fierce animal.

imagery: a combined term for figurative language in the form of simile, metaphor or personification.

irony: saying the opposite of what you really mean for humorous effect; *or* a twist of fate in events, such as the occurrence of an unexpected coincidence.

jargon: technical language or language that is used by specialists of some kind.

juxtaposition: placing one thing beside another to create an effect, such as contrast.

linear structure: events in a text take place in order of time.

link: in Close Reading, a sentence (or sentences) which refers both to the idea just discussed and introduces the next one; any joining device in a text.

metaphor: a comparison where one thing is said to *be* another.

oxymoron: a phrase containing opposites: 'frozen fire'.

paradox: an apparent contradiction of ideas, e.g. 'you must be cruel to be kind'.

personal: writing that refers to the writer's own experience and feelings, often in the first person; the personality of the writer will be clearly evident. (In the case of impersonal writing, the opposite will apply.)

personification: an inanimate object is spoken of as if it has a mind of its own.

register: a form of language used in restricted circumstances, e.g. formal language; medical terminology.

sentence structure: how words are arranged in a sentence, and how elements such as subject, verb, object are arranged. Repetition, antithesis, listing, climax would all be relevant.

setting: where and when the action of a text takes place.

simile: a comparison using 'like' or 'as'.

structure: the way a text is put together (e.g. using flashbacks); the development of ideas in a text.

techniques: a vague expression which is very wide-ranging and may include tone, use of illustration, simile, metaphor, alliteration, personification, hyperbole, sentence structure, repetition, listing, use of comparisons, a personal or impersonal approach, etc.

theme: a main idea put across in a text, e.g. 'winning at all costs'; 'the evils of racism'; 'love conquers all' or 'the abuse of power'.

third person: use of '*he*', 'she', 'it', 'they', as opposed to 'I', 'we' (first person), or 'you' (second person).

tone: the expression of the writer's feelings or attitude to his subject.

word choice: writer's preference for certain words over others which have similar meanings.